MW01040305

LIVING THE SERMON ON THE MOUNT

LIVING THE SERMON ON THE MOUNT

A Practical Hope for
Grace and Deliverance

Glen H. Stassen

JOSSEY-BASS
A Wiley Imprint
www.josseybass.com

Published by Jossey-Bass
A Wiley Imprint
989 Market Street, San Francisco, CA 94103-1741   www.josseybass.com

Jossey-Bass books and products are available through most bookstores. To contact Jossey-Bass directly call our Customer Care Department within the U.S. at 800-956-7739, outside the U.S. at 317-572-3986, or fax 317-572-4002.

Jossey-Bass also publishes its books in a variety of electronic formats. Some content that appears in print may not be available in electronic books.

Library of Congress Cataloging-in-Publication Data
Stassen, Glen Harold, date.
Living the Sermon on the mount: a practical hope for grace and deliverance / Glen H. Stassen.
p. cm. — (Enduring questions in Christian life series)
Includes bibliographical references and index.
ISBN-13: 978-0-7879-7736-8 (cloth)
ISBN-10: 0-7879-7736-5 (cloth)
1. Sermon on the mount. I. Title.
BT380.3.S73 2006
241.5'3—dc22   2006010544
Printed in the United States of America

FIRST EDITION
HB Printing 10 9 8 7 6 5 4 3

ENDURING QUESTIONS IN CHRISTIAN LIFE™

David P. Gushee
SERIES EDITOR

———

Only Human:
Christian Reflections on the
Journey Toward Wholeness
David P. Gushee

Living the Sermon on the Mount:
A Practical Hope for Grace and Deliverance
Glen H. Stassen

Joy in Divine Wisdom:
Practices of Discernment from
Other Cultures and Christian Traditions
Marva Dawn

CONTENTS

E ach book in the Enduring Questions in Christian Life series tackles an essential issue that arises, and has arisen for two thousand years, at the intersection of faith and everyday life. In the first book in this series, I have written about what it means to be human. Coming books by other authors will explore love, discernment, justice, sexuality, and additional themes.

At first glance, a book on the Sermon on the Mount might seem an odd fit for this series. In what sense can it be said that Jesus' most famous sermon is an enduring question in Christian life?

A couple of answers ought to be kept in mind as you read this exciting book by Glen Stassen. One is that of all Jesus' teachings, none has so captured the human (and not just the Christian) imagination. It is not a stretch to say that these three chapters of Matthew in the New Testament have changed the world. They have certainly changed many millions of lives. Different ways to interpret these teachings have circulated pretty much ever since they were offered. So in reading this book you are entering into one of the longest and most important discussions in the whole of Christian history.

This is all true. But the main reason the Sermon on the Mount is an enduring question is how these powerful words of

Jesus pose a set of enduring questions to each of us. This is especially apparent through Stassen's impressive and original interpretation of Jesus' mountaintop address.

Stassen argues that the Sermon on the Mount offers the
best and most complete picture of who Jesus was and what he
was really all about. But Stassen goes on to show that for Jesus
himself the Sermon points not just to him but to the God who
sent him. Ultimately the Sermon paints a picture of a certain
kind of God: one who is present and active in the world, bringing deliverance and healing into our wounded lives and broken
relationships. This is a God who is always doing new things, who
is worthy of our trust and loyalty because of the depth of his
love, mercy, and compassion.

So one question the Sermon poses to us is whether we
really believe in God, and in particular this kind of God. If we
do, then we see that the radical teachings Jesus offers here make
perfect sense. Stassen shows that they are not merely high ideals,
as so many have said, but infinitely realistic both in their diagnosis of the human condition and in their cure. Here Jesus
teaches us to see reality rightly and to adjust our lives accordingly. The payoff can be glorious: liberation to live as we were
made to live rather than bumping against the God-given structure of reality that does not seem to bend to our whims. So the
call of Jesus to peacemaking, forgiveness, and economic simplic-
ity (to name just a few examples) is not some kind of burden-
some ideal but instead a recipe for wholeness and healing in
human relationships at every level.

I wish I could introduce every reader personally to Glen
Stassen. He has been my teacher, and my friend, for more than
twenty years. Let me just tell you one thing about him: I have
known few people, if any, who have sought to live the teachings
of Jesus the way that Glen does. This book is written not by
some dispassionate scholar of biblical interpretation but by a
human being who for decades has believed that the way of Jesus
is the way of *life,* for himself, for all Christians, and for the
world, and he does all he can to live accordingly.

Which raises yet more questions for you, the reader. Do you believe that Jesus knew what he was talking about when he stood on the mountain and offered his famous Sermon? If so, are you living out his teachings? If not, how is the alternative working out for you? Ultimately, *Living the Sermon on the Mount* offers an inviting and compelling summons to a certain kind of life, one rooted in loyalty to the God whose character is revealed by the life, and the teachings, of Jesus himself. I think you will find the book to be remarkably good at asking questions of the kind that get right to the heart of belief—and life.

David P. Gushee
Series Editor

To Howard Rees,

Helen Johnson,

and Dan Williams—

rescuers in my own life-and-death

struggle with faith and doubt.

The Sermon on the Mount begins, "When Jesus saw *the crowds,* he went up the mountain; and after he sat down, *his disciples* came to him. Then he began to speak, and taught them" (Matt. 5:1–2). Did the crowds follow him too, or only the disciples? Did he teach only the disciples, or were the crowds listening in too? Are we invited in, or are only Jesus' close followers invited?

The Sermon on the Mount concludes, "Now when Jesus had finished saying these things, *the crowds were astounded* at his teaching, for he taught them one having authority; and not as their scribes" (Matt. 7:28–29). The crowds were there. They heard and were impressed.

I want to invite you in, whether you are a disciple or not. Literally billions of people have heard or read this phenomenal teaching. Many have said, "Wow!" I hope to make the Sermon on the Mount as clear as I can so that almost anyone can understand it, and live it.

I believe Jesus taught the Sermon on the Mount first of all for his disciples—pupils, learners, students, followers. I want all of us to be at least his learners. I believe the Sermon is God's will for all the people God created. This means all of us are invited to learn from it. This teaching can make your life much more integrated, more reconciled with God, and less frantic and contentious. If you are one of his closer disciples, I hope this book can help you live Jesus' way more fully and explain it to others in a way that makes real sense.

One of the discoveries of this book is how many times Jesus quoted the prophet Isaiah. Whenever he announced the coming of the kingdom of God, which was central to his teaching, he was referring to Isaiah. Whenever he talked about peacemaking, justice, joy, God's presence, or healing, he was often referring to Isaiah.

He quoted Isaiah a lot. Have you ever seen an ancient scroll of a book of the Old Testament? The scrolls of Isaiah would be rolled up on a long, round piece of wood. In mundane picture language, the scrolls are somewhat the shape of a rolling pin, only bigger, perhaps four feet long and almost a foot thick. Precious and holy, they had to be copied meticulously by hand. They were not widely available. Synagogues might have scrolls of a few books of the Old Testament, but not the entire Old Testament. Today they are carefully decorated in a protective sheath and kept behind glass above the altar for protection, while at the same time they can be seen and revered.

We can be sure that Jesus was not carrying around a scroll of Isaiah in his back pocket. As he traveled and taught, Jesus quoted passages from throughout Isaiah, not from only one favorite chapter or two. This means he had memorized Isaiah—or much of Isaiah—studied it deeply, and was immersed in it so that when he taught he regularly cited phrases and verses. Remember Jesus was human like us. He did not have an Isaiah chip implanted in his brain. He studied the book and learned its meaning.

Jesus grew up gradually and learned more as he grew. Obviously, he studied Isaiah, as well as Deuteronomy and Psalms, Genesis, and other books. As Luke tells us, "The child grew and became strong, filled with wisdom; and the favor of God was upon him. . . . And Jesus increased in wisdom and in years, and in divine and human favor" (2:40, 52). When he was twelve, he went with his parents to Passover in Jerusalem. He went to the temple, and was "sitting among the teachers, listening to them and asking them questions. And all who heard him were amazed at his understanding and his answers" (Luke 2:46–47). I am guessing it was Isaiah they were discussing. They were impressed with how well Jesus knew Isaiah, and how insightfully he interpreted Isaiah's writings.

I hope to show that God was also present in Jesus in a unique way. When Jesus spoke and acted, the reign of God was coming through him. But right-believing, traditional, conservative Christian theology is clear that this did not cancel his fully human nature. Jesus was human, as we are; hungry and thirsty as we are; tempted as we sometimes are; and when he was stabbed by the Roman soldiers, he bled as we bleed. He also got angry, and sometimes he called people fools. He confronted the authorities for their various injustices. He was a realist about human nature.

Moreover, Jesus identified his message closely with Isaiah's. He quoted Isaiah far more frequently than any other part of the Bible. He taught that Isaiah was right. He understood his own mission, and Israel's mission, in terms of Isaiah. He taught that God was doing new things through his own healing and teaching, and what those new things meant was articulated by Isaiah; it fulfilled what Isaiah himself had articulated. This is an astoundingly strong affirmation of the prophet Isaiah.

Accordingly, I believe that our interpretation of Jesus' teachings should pay attention to their context in Isaiah. I believe that if we do not see how Jesus' teachings are rooted in the Old Testament, we treat them like flowers that have been pulled out of the soil and displayed in a vase of water. They get thin, or they even lose their real life. Similarly, when the teachings of Jesus are uprooted we plant them again in our own soil. They take on the meaning we put into them, rather than retaining their real meaning. We shape his teachings to fit the distortion of our own interests: greed, militarism, nationalism, racism, individualism, and rationalization of what we wanted to hear Jesus say.

Jesus also quoted Genesis, Deuteronomy, and the Psalms; he referred to Leviticus, Daniel, Ezekiel, Jeremiah, Zechariah, and others. I am not saying he referred only to Isaiah, but Isaiah was a symbol for how deeply rooted Jesus was in the Old Testament, just as we now know that the Dead Sea Scrolls from the Qumran community, which was contemporary with Jesus, quoted from the prophet Isaiah more any other writing.

I am passionate about the ideas I present in this book as to the structure and meaning of Jesus' teaching. One discovery is that the central section of the Sermon on the Mount is fourteen teachings, each made up of three parts. You will see how this discovery makes Jesus' teachings a practical hope for grace and deliverance, much more than other past interpretations that did not do so. Biblical writers such as Matthew loved numbers that symbolized completeness and goodness: three, seven, three times fourteen. So the Gospel of Matthew begins with three times fourteen generations from Abraham to Jesus, and the main section of the Sermon on the Mount is fourteen teachings, each with three parts.

The most respected scholarly journal for biblical studies, *The Journal of Biblical Literature,* published my technical evidence for this interpretation of the Sermon on the Mount as the longest article I have ever seen in the journal. It means many scholars are saying yes to these new discoveries that make the Sermon on the Mount so practical for daily living. This might boost your confidence as you read this simple book.

My goal is to make the Sermon on the Mount just as clear as I can. I try to avoid getting bogged down in technical debate with the scholars. I just want to make this teaching plain. That's easy for me, because I am a rather plain and ordinary person myself, the grandson of an immigrant tomato farmer in Minnesota. What Minnesotans most hate is people who put on airs. Among my parents and my fifteen aunts and uncles, only one went to college. I have been a farmworker, a paper boy, a caddy, a construction-crew laborer, a factory laborer, a dorm counselor, a physicist, an electronics engineer, a youth minister, a pastor, and a teacher. So I have gotten to know a lot of everyday people with everyday-people questions, worries, and laughs.

I am also a disciple, a learner. Although I have not loaded the book with scholarly footnotes, there are many scholars I should thank. I owe my first approach to this subject to teachers W. W. Adams and W. D. Davies. I especially want to thank Dale Allison and Richard Hays for their more recent help. I deeply wish I could personally thank Howard Rees and Helen Johnson of the Washington, D.C., student study group; they taught me what overshadowed by Jesus' powerful love means personally and experientially, and rescued my faith. I owe them far more than they knew. I thank Scott Becker for our co-authored article on which I based part of Chapter Ten, and for creating the index. Finally, I want to thank Sheryl Fullerton, Thomas Finnegan, and David P. Gushee, whose active editing has made *Living the Sermon on the Mount* more pleasant to read. I have learned much from them.

Although I do not cite scholars much, I want to assure you that I write with respectful discipleship. I have studied them deeply, and I owe the best scholarship far more than a readable book like this can show. My interpretation is not merely spur-of-the-moment, off-the-top-of-my-head ideas. I have worked hard to be as faithful as I can to what Jesus reveals in the Sermon on the Mount, and to learn from the best teachers.

I hope you will give thanks too, if this simple book makes the way of Jesus plain for you. Not only plain, but practical for your living, and important in freeing you from being stuck in the vicious cycles that trap us in our lives.

Many readers might want to recommend studying this message of deliverance in study groups or church groups. They might find it convenient to divide the book into thirteen sessions in order to meet for three months. In that case, I recommend dividing chapters 3, 4, and 5 in half at pages 51, 71, and 98, respectively. These half-chapters have plenty of meat for discussion, and they set the pattern for the following chapters. Once you have understood these half-chapters carefully, the remaining chapters will track readily, because you will have the pattern clearly in mind that the remaining chapters follow.

Seeking God's
Holy Presence
on the Mountain

———

Most of us familiar with the Sermon on the Mount don't give much thought to why Jesus delivered it there—on a mountain. Couldn't it just as easily have been the Sermon on the Plain? Or the Sermon on the Beach? After all, just before the Sermon on the Mount, Matthew tells us, Jesus was walking beside the Sea of Galilee; that's where he encountered Simon and his brother Andrew, as well as James and John, and called them all to follow him. Why does Matthew say he went "up the mountain"?

As with many of the stories in the New Testament that have to do with Jesus and his divinity, Matthew wanted those who heard or read this Gospel to think of parallels in ancient scriptures and connect them to what God is doing here, in and through Jesus. In this case, Jesus going up the mountain intentionally reminds us of Moses going up Mount Sinai to get the Ten Commandments. Moses' story in the book of Exodus begins with his birth and proceeds to his rescue from Pharaoh's murderousness. Jesus' story in the Gospel of Matthew begins with his birth and then relates his rescue from King Herod's murderousness. Moses had to be rescued from Pharaoh's intention to have Jewish boy babies killed, and Jesus and his parents had to flee from Herod's doing the same. Moses and the people of Israel were sojourners in Egypt and then returned to Israel. Jesus and his parents spent a sojourn in Egypt and then returned to Israel. Moses and his people spent forty years in the wilderness before entering into Israel. Jesus fasted forty days in the wilderness before entering into his ministry. Through Moses, God gave the people of Israel the Ten Commandments. Through Jesus, God gave the people of Israel the Sermon on the Mount. Moses was the first prophet in Israel. Jesus and John the Baptist restarted prophecy in Israel after there been no prophets for many years. In all these ways, Matthew tells us that Jesus is renewing and fulfilling the line of prophets who speak God's word to us. Moses began that line of prophets; Jesus is in this sense the new Moses—and more.[1]

THE PRESENCE OF GOD ON THE MOUNTAIN

And here is the point: For Moses, as for Jesus, going up the mountain was about going *into the presence of God,* where God gave him the Ten Commandments, which as we'll see are not just rules and laws but a sign of God's just and merciful deliverance for his vulnerable people.[2] In Exodus 24 and 34, we read that when Moses went up the mountain he was in the presence of God, and God spoke to him. When Jesus "went up the mountain" at the beginning of the Sermon on the Mount, it means that just as Moses went into the presence of God and God spoke to him and Moses delivered God's word to the people, here Jesus brings us into the presence of God and God speaks to us through Jesus. As the outstanding New Testament scholar Ulrich Luz has observed, "The Sermon on the Mount is *Jesus'* sermon; in it Jesus the Son of God speaks, through whom God guarantees the truth of his claim."[3]

GOD'S HOLY NAME—OUR DELIVERER

To be in God's presence is to be in the presence of the one who redeems us, *who delivers us.* This is certainly the case in Exodus 3 and 6, when *the hallowed name of God* is revealed to Moses, and it means "God is our deliverer." It tells us that Yahweh (the Lord) is the one who *delivered* our forefathers, Abraham, Isaac, and Jacob, when they needed deliverance; Yahweh is the Lord who hears our cries and sees our needs when we need deliverance; Yahweh is the Lord who promises to deliver us from our slavery to oppressive powers; and the Lord delivers on his promises. He did in fact deliver our historical predecessors, the people of Israel, from bondage in Egyptian slavery, and after having delivered us, he now reminds us that he is, as the prophet Isaiah says again and again, "The Holy One of Israel, our *Redeemer,*" our Deliverer.

How does God redeem us? Though we do not usually think of the Ten Commandments as deliverance for those who are vulnerable but more as strict rules of conduct, this is God's intention. The one who gives us the Ten Commandments is the Holy Lord *who delivers us,* the Lord who hears our cries, sees our needs, and delivers us from our need and our slavery—as the Lord did in Egypt. This is why the Ten Commandments begin, "I am the Lord your God, who brought you out of the land of Egypt, out of the house of slavery." This is also why the first three commandments make clear that we shall not have any other gods before the Lord; why God is revealed in the deliverance from slavery and not in some idol that we make for ourselves; and why we shall not make wrongful use of the hallowed "name of the Lord your God, for the Lord will not acquit anyone who misuses his name" (Exod. 20:3–7).

The rest of the commandments continue in this way to deliver those who are vulnerable and in need of deliverance. All workers—including slaves, animals, and immigrants—need a

Sabbath day of rest each week to deliver them from their vulnerability to being overworked. Elderly parents who are vulnerable to neglect must be honored. People who are vulnerable to being murdered need a society that protects them from murder. Married persons who are vulnerable to betrayal and the destruction of marriage require protection from adultery. People who are vulnerable to stealing (originally this was a prohibition against kidnapping) should have protection from stealing. People who are being tried in a law court or whose reputation is being threatened must be protected from false witness. Neighbors need protection from other neighbors who might covet and steal their possessions. The Ten Commandments are about God's deliverance of the vulnerable from powerful forces that threaten them; they are also about God's command to us to participate in delivering those who are vulnerable.

If you are at the wrong end of a gun and vulnerable to being killed, you feel vulnerable and needy, and you appreciate the compassion of God who hears cries, sees needs, and delivers from bondage. You appreciate a covenant community that works together to reduce homicide and protect people from being killed. If you are an elderly parent who is alone in a retirement home, you greatly appreciate children who are thoughtful enough to come visit you regularly. If your reputation is being cheapened by gossip, you appreciate God giving us biblical teachings against false witness, gossip, and slander. The Lord, the Holy Redeemer of Israel, hears our cries and brings deliverance. The Ten Commandments are about God's presence, and God's delivering love for the vulnerable.

JESUS' MESSAGE OF DELIVERANCE

So is the Sermon on the Mount. In his Sermon on the Mount, Jesus gives a way of deliverance for a people who need it just as desperately as their ancestors did when Moses led them out of

Egypt. On the mountain, Jesus brings the message that the kingdom of God or reign of God is at hand—is becoming present. The presence of God is important, good news for the people of Israel who were hearing Jesus' message because there had been no prophets for many years. In some of the most recent writings before Jesus came, such as Ecclesiastes, it seemed that God was not very present, not doing anything new. As the writer of Ecclesiastes says, nothing new is happening under the sun.

> Vanity of vanities! All is vanity.
> What do people gain from all the toil
>   at which they toil under the sun? . . .
> What has been is what will be,
> and what has been done is what will be done;
> there is nothing new under the sun [Eccles. 1:2–3, 9].

Ecclesiastes was probably written about two hundred or three hundred years before Jesus. Other books such as Tobit were written still later; they are called apocryphal or deuterocanonical books in some Bibles—often between the Old and New Testaments. They seem to suggest that people of the time did not sense God doing new things; instead, angels and magic caused things to happen. Or when God was seen as active, as in Judas Maccabeus' uprising, God was seen as supporting a nationalistic war, which led to disaster and disillusionment. Though not all scholars agree on this interpretation, it seems to me that after the close of the Old Testament and before the coming of Jesus, the literature of the time shows that people did not have the sense of God's dynamic presence that we see in the prophets. They were under the domination of the Roman Empire, and they were disheartened by moral compromise and moral corruption. They longed for God's return, for deliverance from the domination of the Roman Empire.

It is easy to imagine how so many welcomed John the Baptist and his proclamation that the reign of God is now at hand, that Israel has a prophet again. Jesus, baptized by John, takes up the proclamation, telling all who have ears to hear that the reign of God is at hand. In his teachings, and particularly in the Sermon on the Mount, Jesus tells us that God is speaking again, coming to be present again and to deliver us. God is coming to deliver us from our vicious cycles of anger and violence, unfaithfulness and adultery, manipulation and deceit, materialism and greed—and our double-mindedness, from our separation from God.

In the twenty-first century, we may be living in a time similar to that period before Jesus. We are living in what I think of as the backwash of the seventeenth-century Enlightenment (and the centuries following it), when it was thought that God does not do anything new because everything is determined by universal and fixed laws of physics. The Enlightenment, also known as the Age of Reason, is symbolized by Sir Isaac Newton's laws of physics, which described and determined the workings of the natural world. In Newton's view, atoms were like self-contained billiard balls rotating around each other according to preexisting and absolute physical laws. The philosopher Pierre Simon de Laplace even wrote that if we could know where all the particles are at one moment, and what direction they were going and how fast, we could predict the future of everything. If everything obeys fixed laws, "there is nothing new under the sun." There is no room in this fixed and closed universe for God to do anything new. Human beings—emotions, thoughts, bodies, actions—are but electrons obeying fixed laws. Our lives are determined by the laws of physics.

People believed this because clearly physics was able to explain much that happened at the level where it specialized (the movement of physical forces and objects). Its knowledge led to new physical discoveries and machines. Other disciplines, from chemistry to psychology and economics, tried to develop a similar kind of logic at the level where they each focused. The result was to reduce understanding of complex dimensions of life to fixed laws about basic elements. In this world of mechanical laws and behavioristic psychology, who are we ourselves? Only the products of impersonal forces? With no room for God to create anything new?

My own undergraduate major was nuclear physics. I had a daydream of myself being reduced to nothing but a brain floating in a large bowl of chemicals, connected to mechanical arms by radio waves from the brain. But I realized that even the thoughts in my brain were grounded in the movement of electrons, which obey the laws of physics, so even my thoughts were predetermined by the laws of physics.

But now we know better. New discoveries such as quantum physics, wave theory, quarks and other particles in the nucleus, Heisenberg's uncertainty principle, and Einstein's theory of relativity have opened up freedom in the most basic realities of life. Atoms are not self-contained billiard balls obeying fixed laws; they are more like clouds of energy, definitely not fixed. Now and then, basic elements transform into bursts of energy, and there is no predicting when they will do so. The basic building blocks of reality are fluid, open, and full of surprises.

There is much more to all of this, more than we can go into here. The upshot is that the world is not predetermined and closed, as Laplace thought.

So the universe is always changing. We live in an open universe. Life is full of surprises; God is always doing new things. In faith we experience that the new things God does bring us deliverance and the opportunity to participate in God's kingdom. We now live in a post-Newtonian time in which we can celebrate daily the new gifts that God bestows on our lives. It is time to open up to God's presence.

Recently my wife was gone for about three weeks, helping her brother and sister-in-law in the library of the International Baptist Theological Seminary in Prague. I was lonely, and a strained relationship in my own community was bothering me seriously. I was not only lonely but depressed—not clinically, but depressed off and on for several weeks. Then one day, while I was thinking about Jesus' teaching on God's presence, I practiced listening prayer. I did not ask God for things; I just listened for God's word. It came to me just to be grateful that God is present in my loneliness, in the midst of my life. I just meditated on this presence. I sensed the presence of the Holy Spirit, breathing in me with every breath I breathed. I was not alone: God's Holy Spirit was present with me, over me, in me, around me. Lo and behold, my depression lifted. And it stayed lifted.

In telling this story, I want to be careful about what I am saying and not saying. Sometimes depression is caused by chemical imbalance, or by other causes that are very complex. I am not saying that everyone can meditate on God's presence amid loneliness, or that all depression will automatically be lifted. But God's delivering presence is good news, and available to us. I am giving my firsthand testimony; it means very much to me.

I believe this sense of God's presence is a crucial dimension of Jesus' proclamation that the kingdom of God is at hand. It is crucial for interpreting the Sermon on the Mount rightly. The Sermon on the Mount is not first of all about what *we should do*. It is first of all about what *God is already doing*. It is about God's presence, the breakthrough of God's kingdom in Jesus. It is about God's grace, God's loving deliverance *from* various kinds of bondage in the vicious cycles that we get stuck in, and deliverance *into* community with God and others.

GOD'S DELIVERING PRESENCE FULFILLS ISAIAH'S PROPHECIES

In the verses in Matthew before the Sermon on the Mount, this emphasis on God's presence as Deliverer is expressed in three themes: God's presence as Holy Spirit, doing something new; God's delivering justice; and fulfillment of the prophet Isaiah, all happening in Jesus.

The text in Matthew 1:18–25 twice emphasizes the presence of God in the Holy Spirit doing something new: First, Jesus' mother Mary "was found to be with child from the Holy

Spirit." Second, an angel of the Lord said to Joseph in a dream, "the child conceived in her is from the Holy Spirit." Furthermore, twice we are told God is present in Jesus; "they shall name him Emmanuel," and this means "God is with us." In the incarnation of Jesus as a human being, God does something new here. This introductory verse and Matthew's concluding verse ("I am with you always, to the close of the age") serve as bookends, indicating a central theme of the whole Gospel: God's presence.

This same set of verses also strongly emphasizes God's delivering justice working in and through Joseph: Joseph "was just and did not want to cause disgrace for Mary" or expose her to contempt or public disgrace. In verse 24, "he did what the angel of the Lord had commanded and took her to himself," thus delivering her from the disgrace of being pregnant alone. In contemporary culture, many have split the emphasis on justice from the emphasis on God's presence as Holy Spirit. They have also split off salvation from justice. The result is pious people who think they are on God's side even while doing nothing to prevent injustice (or helping cause it). Or they support injustice even as they cover it up with pious talk about God and salvation. But the Bible does not split them; it says again and again that God is a God of compassion who cares deeply about justice, and about delivering people from injustice. This passage clearly puts them together as one united action of God, a new action of deliverance, justice, and presence through the Holy Spirit.

Jesus is also clearly the fulfillment of Isaiah's prophecies: "'She will bear a son, and you are to name him Jesus (which means "Yahweh is salvation"), for he will save his people from their sins.' All this took place to fulfill what had been spoken by the Lord through the prophet: 'Look, the virgin shall conceive and bear a son, and they shall name him Emmanuel,' which means, 'God is with us.'" This is a quote from Isaiah 7:14, which is being fulfilled in Jesus. Isaiah strongly emphasizes God as "the Holy One of Israel, our Redeemer," whose redeeming action

very much includes delivering us from the world's injustice.
Isaiah also emphasizes the Exodus led by Moses and the hope
for a new exodus, a new deliverance, with justice, as we discuss
in the next chapter. We see in this passage the three themes
mentioned at the start of this section: God's presence as Holy
Spirit, doing something new; God's delivering justice; and fulfillment of the prophet Isaiah, all happening in Jesus.

These three themes are likewise present in John the Baptist's announcement of the reign of God. His message was
"Repent, for the kingdom of heaven has come near." John the
Baptist fulfills the prophet Isaiah's prediction: "The voice of one
crying out in the wilderness: Prepare the way of the Lord, make
his paths straight" (Matt. 3:2–3, quoting Isa. 40:3). To "make his
paths straight" is to make justice happen, the kind of justice that
delivers those who are separated from God's way, that brings
them back to God. When John the Baptist talks about the kingdom of heaven, he means God's reign, God's delivering presence. Similarly, John says the one who is coming (Jesus) "will
baptize you with the Holy Spirit and with fire"—clearly indicating the presence of God, in deliverance and in judgment.
When Jesus is baptized, "the heavens opened to him, and he saw
the Spirit of God descending like a dove and alighting on him"
(Matt. 3:16). The Holy Spirit speaks the words of Isaiah 42:1:
"'This is my Son, the Beloved, with whom I am well pleased'"
(Matt. 3:17). John calls on the Pharisees and Sadducees to "bring
fruit which corresponds to repentance," which means to do justice that fits God's will.[4] The form that this justice should take
is clarified in Luke 3:10–14: "Whoever has two coats must share
with anyone who has none; and whoever has food must do likewise." Tax collectors should "collect no more than the amount
prescribed." Soldiers should "not extort money from anyone by
threats or false accusation." Jesus insists on being baptized by John
in order "to fulfill all righteousness," which means "all justice."

These themes of deliverance and justice continue in
Matthew's telling of Jesus' temptations: "Then Jesus was led up
by the Spirit into the wilderness to be tempted by the devil."

The Spirit is God's presence. Jesus replies to each temptation by quoting Deuteronomy on obeying and serving the Lord, which means doing justice and righteousness. Jesus is delivered from the tempter.

When Jesus goes across the Jordan River to the land of Zebulun and Naphtali, to Galilee of the Gentiles, Matthew tells us that the people there, who have been "living in darkness, have seen a great light, and for those who sat in the region and shadow of death light has dawned" (Matt. 4:13–16). This is a quotation from Isaiah 8:23–9:1. In Isaiah, light and the dawning of light signify the presence of God, God's coming deliverance (Isa. 9:2, 42:6, 49:6, 51:4). The German New Testament scholar Gerhard Lohfink states the meaning of this passage: "Precisely in Galilee, interwoven with Gentiles, the bright light of God is now shining through Israel to the Gentiles. We should see this as the introduction to the Sermon on the Mount."[5] Each of the teaching sections in Matthew has an introduction like this. Again, all three themes are here: presence (light), deliverance, and fulfillment of Isaiah.

In Matthew 4:18–22, when Jesus calls four disciples to follow him, this too is an act of God's presence: it surprises them and brings them into participation in the coming of God's reign. Likewise, we are all called to become participants by becoming followers of Jesus. Being called to become followers of Jesus is the good news of participating in the kingdom.

The emphasis on God's presence as Deliverer is also seen in Jesus' fulfilling Isaiah's prophecies that the Redeemer will come to all of Israel and will bring healing.

AN ALL-ENCOMPASSING AND HEALING PRESENCE

In verses 4:23–24, Matthew uses two Greek words for "all" five times to emphasize the overall inclusiveness of Jesus' works: "Jesus went about in *all* Galilee, teaching in their synagogues and proclaiming the good news of the kingdom and curing *every* disease and *every* sickness among the people. So his fame spread throughout *all* Syria, and they brought to him *all* the sick, those who were afflicted with various diseases and pains, demoniacs, epileptics, and paralytics, and he cured them. And great crowds followed him from Galilee, the Decapolis, Jerusalem, Judea, and from beyond the Jordan" [NRSV translation, my modification].

In naming these places, Matthew describes the whole of Israel: the northwest (Galilee), the northeast (Decapolis), the southwest (Jerusalem and Judea), and the southeast (beyond the Jordan). This too is a fulfillment of Isaiah and a sign of God's delivering presence to all of Israel.[6]

The healing of all kinds of disease and affliction also shows God's delivering presence for all who come to Jesus. It is not, as we often think, about being worthy, about living a perfect life in order to deserve God's blessings. It is about God's love and deliverance shown in Jesus. Jesus' actions, poured out on *all* who come to him and *all* he encounters, foreshadow the spirit and message of the Sermon on the Mount. Blessings are already happening. The healing is already occurring. The Sermon on the Mount is based on God's grace, on God becoming present, delivering, healing, and calling us to participate; it is not based on our being highly moral or perfect.

My good friend Parush Parushev has described a personal experience of healing that perfectly illustrates this all-encompassing outpouring of God's presence and healing.[7] Parush was a Communist, with a Ph.D. in applied mathematics, who had taught math in several leading universities of Europe. While teaching in Poland, Parush got to know a group of Christians and was so moved by what Jesus meant in their lives that he was converted to become a follower of Jesus himself. He returned to his home country of Bulgaria and soon received invitations to preach the good news of Jesus in various churches. With his background, you can imagine he had some of that skeptical backwash from the Enlightenment I mentioned earlier; it is part of what makes the experience so extraordinary for my friend and others who participated.

One day Parush received an urgent call from the pastor of a gypsy village, who asked him to come pray over the sick body of a dying woman and anoint it with oil. They urged them to hurry because she was expected to die any moment. A growing crowd of mourners followed them as they approached the woman's home. The gypsies' custom is to wail with loud, high-pitched cries as someone is dying, and the wailing increased in volume and intensity as the crowd grew. Parush's own words best convey the story from here:

> My heart echoed the mourners' pain with great trembling. This was the first time since my ordination that I was called to minister to a dying person.
>
> The sight evoked my compassion. The woman was lying on one side. I could see the effect the illness had had on her. Her facial features resembled a skull. Her skin was transparent and so tight up around the bones that it felt painful to look at it. The color of her face and hands was turning dark blue. Her stomach was enormously swollen. It was obvious that the life in that body was fading fast. . . .
>
> The procedure of anointing was short. Short, also, was the prayer that followed. In an instant, with my eyes closed, I lost balance. I reached for support and I leaned over, trying to hold onto the iron bed frame. Instead, my hand touched the woman's leg through the cover. The coldness I felt pierced me. In the midst of the summer heat, the woman's limb lay cold and hard as granite. Terrified, I stood there in tears, helpless before the signs of the coming death.
>
> The woman made an attempt to talk; I approached the bed and leaned closer to hear. Her effort caused her mouth to arch, but it gave no sound. . . .
>
> [A sister had] told me that the sick woman had had a dream. She dreamt that I would come, pray for her and

anoint her. After that, she would drink the water of a liter-and-a-half bottle, she would throw it up, and with this she would be completely healed. . . .

I observed in disbelief how the woman gathered what appeared to be her last traces of strength, how she lifted her head and drank the water slowly until the whole amount was consumed. A violent regurgitation followed after. . . .

Each woman present at the scene knew what to do to ensure that all would happen according to the dream. Their faith in the healing power of God stood against my rational mind. Their world, simple and modest, remained unshaken. My world, well built and sophisticated, was crumbling under me.

The transformation was immediate. Before our eyes, the sick woman sat on the bed. We observed how her skin regained its color and her limbs their flexibility. She spoke with a clear voice. She told us that she needed to use the bathroom. The woman got up, all by herself, and headed to the front door. (In those villages, the bathrooms are located outside.) When she appeared in the doorframe, a loud scream of "Ghost!" ripped the skies. The gathered crowd scattered in fear. . . .

Some witnesses of this event were believers. Some were about to become believers. The power of the Spirit pervaded the place. The love of the Lord enveloped it. One by one, all souls joined in giving praise. The mouths of the meek proclaimed His name. . . .

The doctors had given up efforts to fight the disease. The desperately ill woman had been transferred from the local hospital to the capital's fine medical facilities in hope of help. The doctors repeatedly had drained the accumulated liquid in her stomach, but with time this procedure was not efficient anymore. The woman was sent home to die in peace among her family.

Today, the woman is alive and well.

One thing is certainly clear: This is not a story about moral perfection, or about living up to high ideals, or about human moral effort. It is a story about the presence of God, about God doing a new thing, about God bringing deliverance. This is how Matthew introduces the Sermon on the Mount: not as a story about human effort but about the presence of God, bringing deliverance.

Not all experiences of healing are so dramatic; nevertheless they occur. When our son David was a baby, he had a hole between two compartments in his heart, and a valve that wasn't working well between the heart and his main pulmonary artery. These could be repaired by surgery. But he also had a narrowing of the main pulmonary artery that could be repaired only temporarily. In the long run, it was unavoidably life-threatening. We prayed a lot—and worried a lot. So did his doctor. But when the surgeon repaired the hole and the valve, the artery straightened out "all by itself." Everything works well now.

I'm not claiming that David's healing was an unexplainable miracle. Probably after the heart started working properly the artery could also function well. What I am claiming is that even ordinary healing is a gift from God. Every breath we breathe is a gift from God. God does new things all the time.

And God did something special in Jesus. This is how Matthew sets up the beginning of the Sermon on the Mount, and it is why we have spent most of this chapter looking at how these passages show us that God is about presence, deliverance, and healing. Let us not interpret the Sermon on the Mount as it has been interpreted so often: part of the story of Greek idealism, human effort to make ourselves perfect and live up to what seem like impossibly high ideals. Matthew shows as clearly as possible that the Sermon on the Mount needs to be interpreted as the good news of God becoming present to us in Jesus, doing something new; as God's delivering justice breaking through in Jesus; as disciples receiving the gracious call to become followers of Jesus, and people being healed; and as fulfillment of the prophecies of the prophet Isaiah.

Many in our culture (Christians and non-Christians) think of the Sermon on the Mount as high ideals or hard teachings. They admire it from a distance. Indeed, from a distance it does look like high ideals to be striven for by extraordinary effort. But holding at a distance and straining toward impossible standards of perfection are not what Jesus teaches here. Such an approach may indeed be another aspect of the backwash from the Enlightenment, because it does not expect God to do new things. If we believe living these teachings is about our own effort alone, of course it looks morally strenuous. This is not how the disciples saw it. They did not admire it from a distance. Jesus called them, and *immediately* they followed him. They just dropped their fishing nets and followed. They understood Jesus' way from within, as participants. From within, it was good news. It still is, if it is understood rightly.

Our preliminary explorations of the context leading up to the Sermon on the Mount already point us to the truth that the Christian life is not just hard human effort to live up to high ideals; nor is it just a bunch of duties. It is about God's grace. It is about living in the presence of God. It is the invitation of Jesus to participate in the new things God is doing all the time. We are allowed, privileged, and invited to respond to the call of Jesus to follow him as he shows us how to act in the way that fits with what God is doing in our midst. This is what I hope to show as we make our way through the wonders of Jesus' teaching of the Sermon on the Mount. I hope by the end that you can say with me, "Praise God! God is doing something new here! And I can have a part in what God is doing!"

2

Participating with Joy in the Reign of God

The reign of God is coming. We can experience the joy of being part of it; this is what the nine beatitudes in Matthew 5:3–12 say. The first and eighth specifically name the kingdom of heaven and say we can be part of it: "Blessed are the poor in spirit, for theirs is the kingdom of heaven. . . . Blessed are those who are persecuted for righteousness' sake, for theirs is the kingdom of heaven." The others also point to the reality of the reign of God: we will be comforted, will be filled, will inherit the earth, will receive mercy, will see God, will be called children of God. These are descriptions of the coming of God's reign, God's kingdom.

But what does Matthew mean when he talks about God's kingdom, God's reign? It is a phrase so commonly used in Christian circles that it's taken for granted, a fact that may actually hinder full and accurate understanding of the beatitudes and what they really mean, what they imply for our lives together. Before we start to delve more deeply into each one, let's take the time and space to look to Isaiah to clarify the characteristics of the kingdom of heaven, or kingdom of God.

THE KINGDOM OF HEAVEN

Scholars agree that "the kingdom of heaven" means the same reality in the Gospel of Matthew as in the Gospels of Mark and

Luke, when they say "the kingdom of God." The difference is simply that Matthew is a Jew writing for Jewish Christians, where the name of God is too holy to be expressed often; consequently Jews substituted the word *heaven* for *God*. Matthew means what Mark and Luke mean: the kingdom of God.

Scholars also agree that the kingdom of God in Jesus' teaching is not a place, like the Kingdom of Monaco, but a happening. It means God's reign, God's presence, God's coming to deliver us and reign over us. In our present-day language, it is probably clearer to speak of "the reign of God."

Jesus' language about reigning did not mean that Israel would rule over other nations, or that any human empire with a king would be established over other nations. He meant that God was coming to redeem or deliver us from our present mess and would reign instead. In the oppressive Roman Empire of the time, its administrators (Herod and Pilate) and the high priest and temple authorities in Jerusalem, were allowed to rule daily life. Many people probably understood the reign of God in part as deliverance from the reign of the Roman emperor and oppression by the temple authorities. Jesus said that the reign of God will not be about domination but about mutual servanthood (Mark 10:41–45).

Some people make the mistake of splitting life into two realms: the temporal and political on the one hand, which supposedly do not concern Jesus, and the world of "religious" things on the other, which do matter to Jesus. But this makes Jesus' teaching mostly irrelevant for much of life. Jesus did not split life in that way. His distinction was not between political and religious but between domination and mutual servanthood. He also confronted political authorities for dominating unjustly instead of serving, as we shall see later. Jesus was a good Jew: He affirmed that God is Lord over *all* of life, not just religious or inner or individual or spiritual life. This does not mean Christians would establish a Christian empire over other nations any more than it meant Israel would establish an Israeli empire over all the others.

Just before Jesus taught the Sermon on the Mount, John the Baptist came proclaiming the reign of God. Jesus did the same thing in his preaching as well. Now, in the Sermon on the Mount, the first and eighth beatitudes proclaim the kingdom of heaven. In fact, the Sermon on the Mount has three more mentions of the kingdom of heaven. The second petition of the Lord's Prayer is "Your kingdom come"; Matthew 6:33 calls on us to "seek first the kingdom of God"; and in the climax of the Sermon on the Mount, Jesus speaks of entering the kingdom of heaven (7:21).

Beyond the Sermon on the Mount, forty-three more times in the Gospel of Matthew, Jesus speaks of the kingdom. Scholars agree that the central witness and theme of the Synoptic Gospels (Matthew, Mark, and Luke) is that Jesus' mission and message was "the good news of the kingdom of God."[1] But despite emphasis on and frequent references to it in scripture, the big puzzle and important questions (then as well as now) are: What are the characteristics of the reign of God? How do we recognize it when we experience it? How do we know it when we see it? How do our lives fit into it?

Some people spend much time asking another question: When is it coming? But in both Matthew and Mark, Jesus says no one knows when the kingdom will come. "But about that day or hour no one knows, neither the angels in heaven, nor the Son, but only the Father. Beware, keep alert; for you do not know when the time will come" (Mark 13:32). "But about that day and hour no one knows, neither the angels of heaven, nor the Son, but only the Father" (Matt. 24:36). In Acts 1:6–8, the disciples, who were often slow learners because he was teaching them new things, and who still thought maybe they could know when it was coming, asked him, "Lord, is this the time when you will restore the kingdom to Israel?" He replied: "It is not for you to know the times or periods that the Father has set by his own authority. But you will receive power when the Holy Spirit has come upon you; and you will be my witnesses in Jerusalem, in all Judea and Samaria, and to the ends of the earth."

What is important, Jesus said, is to do the deeds he teaches so we are ready for it when it comes. If we put our attention on *when* instead of on *what its characteristics are,* we neglect the practices that prepare for it. As the prominent theologian N. T. Wright says in his masterful book on the historical Jesus, "The crucial question is not so much that of the kingdom's *timing* as of its *content*."[2] When he says *content* Wright refers to things such as God's presence, peace, and joy. Debate still rages about the "when question," but the truth is no one—not scholars, not theologians, not church officials—knows. Since Jesus says nobody knows the answer, I do not bother here to discuss the speculative answers that have been put forth, but I do tell a personal story about how people put so much time and energy into figuring it out.

On the first morning of our marriage, a Sunday, Dot and I were driving down the beautiful Blue Ridge Parkway on our honeymoon, heading toward the Great Smoky Mountains of North Carolina. About the time we got to Natural Bridge in southern Virginia, we turned off to spend that important morning going to worship in the first Baptist church we saw. In the church we found, it happened that this Sunday was in the middle of a two-week revival. The whole front of the sanctuary, from wall to wall, was covered by a huge map portraying the exact order of the events that will occur at the end of the world. There were orange lines, purple lines, yellow lines, lilac, brown, green, blue, red, black, and even more colors as well as symbols indicating the timing of all the future events.

The first half of the sermon summarized the events the minister had described the previous week. The second half pointed to the exciting events he would explain in the week to come, in hopes we would all be there to hear about them during the coming week. It was fantastic. I had never seen or heard anything like it.

But the minister gave us no guidance about how we could conduct our lives as followers of Jesus so that they would fit what God was about to do in this sequence of events.

I wondered if it meant something that our marriage was beginning this way. Was the fact that our first worship service as husband and wife focused on the end of the world some kind of omen about our marriage?

We didn't stay the week to find out; we had a reservation in a honeymoon resort in the Great Smoky Mountains. What really mattered to us more than knowing when the end would come was how to build a marriage that is faithful to the reign of God. It had to be a marriage with the presence of God in it, a significant amount of healing, some joy, commitment to working for the kind of peace and justice that God wills, and now and then redemption from error and return to the Lord. The Book of Revelation emphasizes whether we are doing the deeds that Jesus taught, in our marriage and family as well, rather than when everything will happen. The followers of the Lamb do the deeds that Jesus taught (Rev. 2:2, 19, 23, 26; 3:8, 10; 9:20–21; 12:17; 14:4, 12; 16:11; 19:10; 20:12–13; 22:11), and they are delivered from destruction. The Sermon on the Mount gives us the teachings of Jesus about the deeds we are to do so that our light shines and others can see our good works and give glory to our Father in heaven (Matt. 5:16).

Since, as Jesus says, no one knows the timing of the full coming of the reign of God, the key is to be ready. He says we are blessed, because the reign of God is (or will be) ours. What we need is signs or characteristics of what God does in God's reign, so we can participate.

If I ask you to write down the characteristics of the kingdom of God, of the reign of God, what will you write? If you aren't sure, there are places we can look—such as in the prophet Isaiah—to gain some sense of what the kingdom and reign will be like.

WHAT THE PROPHET ISAIAH SAYS

Since the coming of the reign of God was central to Jesus' proclamation, surely it had to be something that the people in Jesus' day understood. The evidence is that what people were reading most in Jesus' time was the prophet Isaiah. Jesus quoted Isaiah whenever he proclaimed the coming of the reign. With only one exception, no other literature in the first century speaks of "the reign of God." Logically, then, to understand what "the reign of God" meant in Jesus' day, we should ask what it meant in the prophet Isaiah.

John the Baptist came proclaiming the reign of God as the fulfillment of Isaiah (Matt. 3:2–3). Then Jesus "began to proclaim, 'Repent, for the kingdom of heaven has come near.'" This also fulfilled the prophet Isaiah (Matt. 4:14–17), as we saw in the last chapter.

The Gospels of Mark and Luke tell us the same thing:

> As it is written in the prophet Isaiah,
> "See, I am sending my messenger ahead of you,
> who will prepare your way;
> the voice of one crying out in the wilderness:
> 'Prepare the way of the Lord, make his paths straight. . . .'"

"Now, after John was arrested, Jesus came to Galilee, proclaiming the good news of God and saying, 'The time is fulfilled, and the kingdom of God has come near; repent, and believe in the good news'" (Mark 1:2–3, 14–15).

He stood up to read, and the scroll of the prophet Isaiah was given to him. He unrolled the scroll and found the place where it was written:

> The Spirit of the Lord is upon me,
> because he has anointed me to bring good news to the poor.
> He has sent me to proclaim release to the captives
> and recovery of sight to the blind,
> to let the oppressed go free,
> to proclaim the year of the Lord's favor. . . .

"Today this scripture has been fulfilled in your hearing. . . . I must proclaim the good news of the kingdom of God to the other cities also; for I was sent for this purpose" (Luke 4:17–19, 21, 43).

The prophet Isaiah was the best-known literature in Jesus' day. The Dead Sea Scrolls, from the Qumran community, which existed at the same time as Jesus, include scrolls of Isaiah but also quote and refer to Isaiah far more than they do any other books. The New Testament quotes and refers to Isaiah much more than to any other prophet. Jesus quotes Isaiah again and again, more than anything else.

Ulrich Luz observes that the Gospel of Matthew seems to have been written in a Christian community split from the synagogue: "In its library, there was a scroll of Isaiah; Isaiah plays the most important role of all prophets—in Matthew, as elsewhere in early Christianity." By contrast, Matthew's quotations from all the rest of the Old Testament seem to have come from memory; there is no evidence his community had a scroll from any of the minor prophets, or any other part of the Old Testament.[3]

Bruce Chilton is an expert in the Greek New Testament and the Aramaic language that Jesus spoke. In Jesus' day, most people no longer used Hebrew; they spoke Aramaic. Chilton studied all the passages concerning Jesus' announcement of the kingdom of God[4] and discovered that in each Jesus refers to the prophet Isaiah in Aramaic translation.[5] Jesus uses words and phrases in his kingdom proclamations from fourteen chapters of Isaiah (24:23, 25:6, 31:6, 40:10, 41:8ff, 42:1, 43:5 and 10, 45:6, 49:12, 51:7–8, 53:1, 59:19, 60:20–22, and 61:1).

Since the Jews of Jesus' time spoke Aramaic, during worship services the rabbi would read the scripture in Hebrew and then a translator, called a *meturgeman,* would paraphrase the Hebrew scripture passage in Aramaic. It was not to be an exact translation but a paraphrase, sort of like a *Good News for First-Century People.* Because Jesus was speaking so people would understand, he regularly referred to Isaiah in Aramaic translation.

In the written paraphrase of Isaiah that gradually came together during the next three centuries, called the "Isaiah Targum," four passages speak directly of "the reign of God," or kingdom of God, and one speaks of "the reign of the Messiah."[6]

All five passages basically say that the presence of God, coming to deliver us, is being revealed before our very eyes. But Jewish piety did not want to say directly that "God is revealed," because God is too holy to be seen. Instead, it was said more indirectly: "The reign of God is revealed." This means the reign or kingdom of God is about the self-revelation of God and God's presence, coming to deliver us. Chilton observes: "Especially in the Targum of Isaiah, the language of the kingdom is employed to render passages that in the Hebrew original speak of God intervening actively on behalf of his people. The emphasis is on the dynamic, personal presence of God—not on the nature of God in itself, but on his saving, normally future activity."[7]

Seventeen passages in Isaiah proclaim the good news of deliverance by God (9:1–7, 11; 24:14–25:12; 26; 31:1–32:20; 33; 35; 40:1–11; 42–44:8; 49; 51:1–52:12; 52:13–53:12; 54; 56; 60; 61; 62). For the most part, these are the same passages that Chilton found Jesus quoting in his kingdom. Jesus therefore proclaims that the reign of God that Isaiah has prophesied is at hand. His reference to Isaiah is not surprising, given that Isaiah was the best-known biblical book in Jesus' day. Many people had memorized much of Isaiah; Jesus certainly had. Jesus chose Isaiah to teach and preach from; he was deeply engaged in Isaiah, and thus affirmed that Isaiah teaches the truth—the most important truth of God's reign.

THE SEVEN CHARACTERISTICS OF THE REIGN OF GOD

The key questions are: What did the reign of God—that Jesus was proclaiming—mean in Isaiah? Are there any themes that run through these seventeen passages in Isaiah that announce the good news of God's deliverance? Do we see themes in these deliverance passages that identify the content and characteristics of God's reign as Jesus proclaimed? The answer to all these questions is yes; there are seven main themes or characteristics that we can see in Isaiah and in Jesus' teachings about the reign of God.

1. *God's presence as Spirit or Light,* in nine passages (God's dynamic presence is implied in all seventeen)
2. *Deliverance or salvation* occurs in all seventeen
3. *Peace* in fourteen
4. *Healing* in seven
5. *Joy* in twelve
6. *Return from exile* occurs in nine (Jesus interprets this as repentance and return to God)
7. *Righteousness or justice* occurs in sixteen passages

It is remarkable how clearly Jesus teaches, fulfills, and enacts all seven characteristics.

GOD'S PRESENCE AS LIGHT AND AS HOLY SPIRIT

Isaiah 60 clearly announces the presence of God. In Isaiah, as well as in Jesus' teaching, darkness is a symbol for God's absence and light is a symbol for God's presence:

> Arise, shine; for your light has come,
> and the glory of the LORD has risen upon you.
> For darkness shall cover the earth,
> and thick darkness the peoples;
> But the LORD will arise upon you,
> and his glory will appear over you. . . .
> The sun shall no longer be your light by day,
> nor for brightness shall the moon give light to you
>   by night,
> but the LORD will be your everlasting light,
> and your God will be your glory [Isa. 60:1–2, 19].

Glory has the meaning of the visible evidence of the splendor, majesty, sovereignty, light, revelation, and presence of God. The opening line ("your light has come, and the glory of the LORD has risen upon you") is a parallelism, typical of Hebrew poetry. It says the same thing in two parallel sets of words: God has come to be present and is revealed to you. It means God will be really present to you.

We also see the theme of God's presence as Spirit and light in other passages: "Here is my servant, whom I uphold, my chosen, in whom my soul delights; I have put my Spirit upon him; he will bring forth justice to the nations" (42:1). "I will turn the darkness before them into light" (42:16). "When you pass through the waters, I will be with you" (43:2). "I will pour my Spirit upon your descendants" (44:3).

All seventeen passages of Isaiah that announce God is coming to deliver us and reign over us include the experience of God's presence, even where they do not directly say *Spirit* or *light*. We will see that in the Sermon on the Mount the active presence of God is the key.

REDEEMING, SAVING, DELIVERING

Isaiah 43:1–4 describes the people of Israel as they are exiled in Babylon. They are oppressed, and the LORD is coming, to create a new Exodus from oppression just as he delivered them once before from slavery in Egypt. The LORD is Redeemer, Savior, and Deliverer; the three terms for deliverance have basically the same meaning. Isaiah teaches us to know God primarily as our Deliverer, Savior, Redeemer, not as the One who stays distant from us because we are sinful. God's *holiness* is revealed not in distance from all sinners but in being with us to redeem us. The LORD *created Israel* not in the creation of Genesis but in the Exodus from Egypt, when the LORD delivered the people from the Pharaoh in Egypt by making a path through the waters of the Sea of Reeds:

But now thus says the LORD,
He who *created* you O Jacob,
He who formed you, O Israel:
"Do not fear, for I have *redeemed* you;
I have called you by name, you are mine.
When you pass through the waters, I will be with you;
And through the rivers they shall not overwhelm
     you. . . .
For *I am the LORD* your God
The Holy One of Israel, your *Savior.* . . .
and I love you."

Notice that the LORD says, "I will be with you." This is what God promised in the revelation of his name as "the LORD"— the "I am" in Exodus 3 and 6—to be *present,* and to *deliver.* The LORD, the "I am," is here, present, and bringing about the *return.*

Notice too that God is present to deliver and enable the people to return, because "I love you." Throughout Isaiah, God's motivation in delivering us, bringing about justice, peace, healing, and return, is God's love, God's compassion. Isaiah says this again and again[8]: "With great compassion I will gather you. . . . With everlasting love I will have compassion on you, says the LORD, your Redeemer" (Isa. 54:7–8). Jesus continues this theme of God's compassion for people in need of deliverance; the Gospels also see this compassion of God revealed in Jesus (Mark 1:41, 6:34, 8:2, 9:22; Matt. 9:36, 14:14, 15:32, 18:27, 20:34; Luke 7:13, 10:33, 15:20). Compassion comes from the word for womb and means a gut feeling of empathy and identification with someone in need. It is like God hearing the cries of the slaves in Egypt, seeing their need, and coming to be present to deliver them. It is one more example of God's action of deliverance in Exodus being central for Isaiah, and Jesus affirming Isaiah's message as central truth. *Compassion* occurs twelve times in the Gospels, though not in other parts of the New Testament. It seems to be a special theme of Jesus' (and Isaiah's) in the first three Gospels but not typical of Paul, John, James, or the other writers. Jesus taught that God is the compassionate One who delivers us, just as Isaiah did.

In Isaiah 43:5–19, God promises to be *present, delivering* and *redeeming,* enabling people to *return,* and bringing *peace*:

> Do not fear, *for I am with you;*
> I will bring your offspring from the east
> and from the west I will gather you;
> I will say to the north, "Give them up,"
> and to the south, "Do not withhold;
> bring my sons from far away
> and my daughters from the end of the earth. . . ."
> I am God, and also henceforth I am He;
> there is no one who can *deliver* from my hand;
> I work, and who can hinder it?
> Thus says the LORD,
> your *Redeemer,* the Holy One of Israel. . . .
> I am the LORD, your Holy One,
> the Creator of Israel, your King.
> Thus says the LORD,
> who makes a way in the sea,
> a path in the mighty waters,
> who brings out chariot and horse,
> army and warrior;
> they lie down; they cannot rise,
> they are extinguished, quenched like a wick. . . .
> I am about to do a new thing;
> now it springs forth, do you not perceive it?
> I will make a way in the wilderness
> and rivers in the desert.

PEACE

Israel and Judah lived on the land bridge between Egypt to the south and Babylon, Syria, Assyria, Babylon, and Persia to the north and northeast. (Babylon and Persia were literally to the east, but because of the barrier of the Arabian desert, the route was around it to the north.) To Israel's west was the Mediterranean Sea, and to its east was the Arabian desert; so during the time of the book of Isaiah Israel and Judah were located on a bridge that the great powers wanted to control. When Israel and Judah practiced greed and injustice and put their trust in weaponry and military alliances with fickle Egypt, instead of following the ways of God, jealousy split them apart. The prophets then pronounced judgment on their foolishness and accurately predicted war and destruction (Isa. 30:1–5, 31:1–3, 32:5–7). First Israel was conquered by Assyria; then Judah was conquered and exiled by Babylon, and eventually released from that exile by Cyrus of Persia when he conquered Babylon. War was a regular threat, and if peace came it would be deliverance from destruction and exile, a return to God's ways of justice, faithfulness, and peacemaking.

In Jesus' day, similar unfaithfulness and foolishness were bubbling up, threatening war with Rome and then destruction of Jerusalem and the temple. Again and again, Jesus predicted Jerusalem and the temple would be destroyed if they did not return to God and practice justice and peacemaking. Even today, the Middle East is a place of injustice, violence, and threats of war. Just as in those ancient days, hope requires a return to the ways of justice and peacemaking.

Isaiah 11:6–13 points the way of hope and calls for repentance from injustice, greed, and jealousy:

> The wolf shall live with the lamb,
> the leopard shall lie down with the kid . . .
> and the weaned child shall put its hand on the
>   adder's den.
> They will not hurt or destroy on all my holy
>   mountain. . . .
> Ephraim shall not be jealous of Judah,
> and Judah shall not be hostile towards Ephraim.

Isaiah 60:17–19 points the way of deliverance:

> I will appoint *Peace* as your overseer
> and *Righteousness* as your taskmaster.
> *Violence* shall no more be heard in your land,
> devastation or destruction within your borders;
> you shall call your walls *Salvation,*
> and your gates *Praise.*

Isaiah 40:1 announces that return from exile will come as peace comes:

> Comfort, comfort my people, says your God.
> Speak tenderly to Jerusalem,
> and cry to her that her warfare is ended. . . . (RSV)

Isaiah 42:2 proclaims that God will bring redemption through the Suffering Servant, who will come with a thorough commitment to nonviolence:

> He will not cry or lift up his voice,
> or make it heard in the street;
> a bruised reed he will not break,
> and a dimly burning wick he will not quench;
> he will faithfully bring forth justice.

Similarly, in Isaiah 53:7–9:

> He was oppressed, and he was afflicted,
> yet he did not open his mouth. . . .
> By a perversion of justice he was taken away. . . .
> although he had done no violence. . . .

HEALING, JOY, AND RETURN

Under the reign of God, God's deliverance will also bring healing, especially healing of the blind. I identify with this promise of healing with special emotion, because one of our own sons is legally blind. David has struggled mightily through many surgeries and much education, overcoming several handicaps. He can now see out of one eye with thick glasses. Now he translates books and articles from the German for graduate students and faculty in theological subjects.

You yourself may have special reason to identify with this because you know someone who needs healing, or who has experienced healing. We can also identify with this promise of healing because we know that Isaiah's proclamation of the coming of the reign of God was fulfilled in Jesus' healing, especially of the blind. Furthermore, in the Gospels Jesus' healing the blind symbolizes the disciples and the people beginning to see and understand that Jesus is the fulfillment of God's promise to redeem them and redeem Israel; Jesus was in fact the coming Deliverer, the Son of God. Many who needed healing were treated as outcasts because of their handicap. When Jesus healed them, he was also restoring them to community:

> Then the eyes of the blind shall be opened.
> And the ears of the deaf unstopped;
> Then the lame shall leap like a deer,
> And the tongue of the speechless sing for joy
>   [Isa. 35:5–6].

Isaiah 42 says:

> I have given you as a covenant to the people,
> A light to the Gentiles,
> To open the eyes that are blind,
> To bring out the prisoners from the dungeon,
> From the darkness those who sit in darkness. . . .
> I will heal the blind by a road they do not know. . . .
> Listen, you that are deaf;
> And you that are blind, look up and see!

The theme of joy occurs when there is healing, deliverance, and often return from exile to Zion and the LORD. For example, consider Isaiah 35:8–10:

A highway shall be there, and it shall be called the
  Holy Way;
the unclean shall not travel on it, but it shall be for
  God's people;
no traveler, not even fools, shall go astray.
And the ransomed of the LORD shall return, and
  come to Zion with singing;
everlasting joy shall be upon their heads;
they shall obtain joy and gladness, and sorrow and
  sighing shall flee away.

JUSTICE AS FAIRNESS AND AS DELIVERANCE

Isaiah 42 is of crucial importance to understanding God's reign.
All three Synoptic Gospels tell us that the Holy Spirit descended
from heaven on Jesus at his baptism and spoke the words of
Isaiah 42:1 (Mark 1:9–11; Matt. 3:13–17; Luke 3:22). This is
Jesus' baptismal passage; it is crucial for declaring his mission.
Notice how strongly it emphasizes the centrality of justice and
confirms the intimate connection of justice with peace and
nonviolence; the servant will not break even a half-broken reed
or quench a barely burning wick. Furthermore, it says clearly
that justice is not only for Israel but inclusively for "the people,"
"the nations," "in the earth"—that is, for the Gentiles. The last
lines promise deliverance to the prisoners, as Jesus does in his
inaugural sermon in Luke 4:18–19. Here is this magnificent passage (Isa. 42:1–7):

Here is my servant, whom I uphold
my chosen, in whom my soul delights;
I have put *my Spirit* upon him;
he will bring forth *justice* to the nations.
He will not cry or lift up his voice,
or make it heard in the street;

a bruised reed he will not break,
and a dimly burning wick he will not quench;
he will faithfully bring forth *justice.*
He will not grow faint or be crushed
until he has established *justice* in the earth;
and the coastlands wait for his teaching.

Isaiah 51:1 and 4–7 confirm these themes, adding that justice
depends on our having God's teaching in our hearts. The passage adds that justice is delivering justice or restorative justice,
not merely punitive justice.

Listen to me, you that pursue *righteousness,*
you that seek the LORD. . . .
Listen to me, my people,
and give heed to me, my nation;
for a teaching will go out from me,
and my *justice for a light to the peoples.*
I will bring near my *deliverance* swiftly,
my *salvation* has gone out
and my arms will rule *the peoples.* . . .
Listen to me, you who know *righteousness,*
you people who have *my teaching in your hearts.* . . .

The reign-of-God passages in Isaiah often place the two words
justice and *righteousness* in parallel because they are meant to translate crucially important Hebrew words that mean almost the
same thing.

The first is *mishpat,* justice in the sense of decisions of the authorities and practices of the markets that are fair to the poor and
the powerless. (Remember from Chapter One that the LORD
is the one who delivered us from Egypt when we were slaves and
vulnerable; the LORD is the one who hears the cries of the
needy and sees their needs and in compassion delivers them.)

The King James Bible translates *mishpat* as "judgment,"
which is right in that it refers to decisions of authorities. But it

does not communicate in English that it equally well refers to economic practices, focusing especially on fairness to the poor and the powerless, the vulnerable. Therefore, most recent versions rightly translate it "justice."

The other word is *tsedaqah,* which means the kind of justice that delivers from slavery and from oppression and restores community relationships.[9] Most translations render *tsedaqah* as "righteousness," which would be correct in biblical culture with its community solidarity. In biblical culture, righteousness meant "delivering justice that restores community relationships." But in our individualistic and possessive culture, most people think of righteousness as a virtue possessed by individuals. That is actually self-righteousness, which the Bible says we cannot have: "There is no one who is righteous, not even one . . . since all have sinned and fall short of the glory of God" (Rom. 3:10, 23, quoting Eccles. 7:20, Ps. 14:1–3, and Isa. 59:7–8).

Instead we should think of "delivering justice that restores community relationships," as in "to bring out the prisoners from the dungeon, from the prison who sit in darkness" (Isa. 42:7, cited earlier). If we need just a two-word translation, wherever we see "righteousness" in the Bible (or "integrity" in the New Jerusalem Bible) we could read "delivering justice" or "restorative justice."

Because *mishpat* means "fairness justice" and *tsedaqah* means "delivering justice," the two words both mean the kind of justice that is fair to the powerless and therefore delivers them from oppression and restores community. This is why the Bible so often puts them in parallel with each other, as we see in Isaiah 42 and 51. Another example is Isaiah 32:1, 15–18:

> See, a king will reign in righteousness,
> and princes will rule with justice. . . .
> Then justice will dwell in the wilderness,
> and righteousness abide in the fruitful field.
> The effect of righteousness will be peace,
> and the result of righteousness, quietness and trust
>   forever.

Here we also see that delivering justice has the effect of creating peace. If people are delivered from injustice and community relationships are restored, they do not need to do violence or make war.

But some people think of justice and righteousness primarily as punishment or retribution, or even as revenge. If that were the meaning, the preceding verse would make no sense. "The effect of *revenge*" is not "peace, quietness, and trust forever" but hatred, resentment, and the drive to strike back. *Tsedaqah* never means punishment in the Bible; there are other words for that. The effect of delivering justice that restores community is indeed peace, quietness, and trust.

For each of the seven characteristics of the reign of God in Isaiah, I have shown only a few examples. But the themes run throughout the seventeen passages. To bring the themes together in one place, let us notice how they are emphasized in Isaiah 9:2–7:

> The people who walked in darkness have seen a
>   great *light*;
> those who dwelt in a land of deep darkness, on them
>   has *light* shined.
> Thou hast multiplied the nation, thou hast increased
>   its *joy*;
> they *rejoice* before thee as with *joy* at the harvest,
> as men *rejoice* when they divide the spoil.
> For the yoke of his burden, and the staff for his
>   shoulder,
> the rod of his oppressor, thou hast broken as on the
>   day of Midian [deliverance].
> For every boot of the tramping warrior in battle
>   tumult
> and every garment rolled in blood will be burned as
>   fuel for the fire [peace].
> For to us a child is born, to us a son is given;
> and the government will be upon his shoulder, and
>   his name will be called,

"Wonderful Counselor, Mighty God, Everlasting
    Father, Prince of *Peace.*"
Of the increase of his government and of *peace* there
    will be no end,
upon the throne of David, and over his *kingdom,* to
    establish it, and to uphold it
with *justice and righteousness* from this time forth and
    for evermore.
The zeal of the Lord of hosts will do this [deliverance].

In Romans 14:17, the Apostle Paul affirms these characteristics
of the kingdom of God. It is highly unusual for Paul to use the
actual phrase "kingdom of God." It is not his usual vocabulary.
He is probably reporting the early Christian understanding that
goes back to Jesus. It is uncanny how strikingly it says just what
we have seen are the characteristics of the kingdom. Paul has
been opposing judgmental arguments about what food we are
allowed to eat (Rom. 14:1–16). In verse 17 he declares: "The
kingdom of God does not mean [arguments about] food and
drink, but *righteousness and peace and joy in the Holy Spirit.*" In
Paul's theology, righteousness has to do with delivering justice,
peace is peace, our joy is in God's salvation, and the Holy Spirit
is God's presence. Here Paul is saying most of what we have
found in the kingdom-of-God passages in Isaiah: the marks of
God's reign are righteousness, peace, joy in God's salvation, and
the presence of God.

Notice how the Christmas story in Luke 1:5–2:20 repeatedly celebrates the *joy* of God's miraculous *presence* and power
acting to bring about the birth of Jesus and the deliverance of
Jews and Gentiles.[10] The words *joy* and *rejoice* occur nine times
in the Greek (sometimes translated as "found favor," "blessed,"
"gladness," or "exulted"). *Peace, justice and righteousness, deliverance
and salvation,* and *kingdom* are declared in the climaxes. Isaiah's
proclamation of *return* is echoed in 1:16, 17, 76; and 3:4–5. *Holy
Spirit* occurs six times, and a revelation of the *presence* of God in

which the angel tells them to fear not as a revelation is received, six times ("The Holy Spirit will come upon you, and the power of the Most High will overshadow you. . . ." I hear in my mind the song "Overshadowed by His Powerful Love"—the key to my own recovery of faith).

Luke 2:22–40 is the story of Simeon and Anna blessing Jesus. Again we see the theme of justice: Simeon was just (*dikaios,* verse 25). Jesus' parents gave the gift of the poor: a pair of turtle doves, or two young pigeons (verse 24). Had they been rich, surely there would have been room for them in the inn. So God's presence to the poor, and deliverance of the poor through Jesus, is clearly symbolized. In Simeon, we see the presence of God as Holy Spirit and light four times; and we see peace, as well as inclusion of the Gentiles. In the prophet Anna's blessing, we hear joyous praise for God's redemption or deliverance of Jerusalem.

The Christmas story is a wonderful celebration of God's delivering grace. It celebrates all the themes of God's coming reign except healing, which will come later.

Christmas is not a sentimental story. It is the historical drama of God's coming and being present to those oppressed and depressed, those poor and marginalized, those who need justice and righteousness and peace, and who need God's presence and God's deliverance. The joy is real; it is presence amid humble reality.

Having now seen the seven characteristics of the reign of God, we are ready to turn to the beatitudes, the first major section of the Sermon on the Mount, and to understand their meaning much more clearly.

The Beatitudes

In this chapter, I show that the beatitudes announce the breakthrough of the reign of God in our midst, with its seven characteristics discussed in Chapter Two. Second, I want to make the meaning of each beatitude clear, digging deeply to get the meaning right, accurate. Third, I want to illustrate the meaning of each beatitude by showing that Jesus' parables illustrate the beatitudes nicely, because the parables teach about the reign of God just as the beatitudes do.

The beatitudes have made such a widespread impression that some people even call the whole Sermon on the Mount (chapters 5 through 7 in Matthew) "the beatitudes." But rightly the beatitudes are the ten verses of Matthew 5:3–12. They are so familiar that they are often taken for granted—and misunderstood. We can see them anew, however, if we go back to what the original Greek says. I have translated them into words that are closer to what I believe, after extensive study, they are really saying:

Joyful are those who are poor and humble before
    God, for theirs is the reign of God.
Joyful are those who are deeply saddened to the
    point of action, for they will be comforted.

Joyful are those whose wills are surrendered to God,
   for they will inherit the earth.
Joyful are those who hunger and thirst for restorative
   justice, for they will be filled.
Joyful are those who practice compassion in action,
   for they will receive God's compassion.
Joyful are those who seek God's will in all that they
   are and do, for they will see God.
Joyful are the peacemakers, for they will be called
   children of God.
Joyful are those who suffer because of restorative
   justice, for theirs is the reign of God.
Joyful are you when they criticize, persecute, and
   slander you, because of me.
Rejoice and be glad, for your reward is great in God.
   For in the same way they persecuted the prophets
   before you.

These teachings are called the beatitudes because they begin with
the Greek word *makarioi* (*beatus* in Latin), meaning blessed, happy,
hopeful, or joyful. I translate *makarioi* as "joyful" because in its
fifty occurrences in the New Testament it almost always means
the joy of participation in God's action of deliverance. In the Old
Testament, it usually promises future consolation to people in
dire straits—meaning, whatever present situation is difficult will
be reversed and justice, peace, and joy will break in. It is not
simply "happy" in the sense of being in an upbeat mood. God is
acting to deliver us, and we have the experience of being part of
what the LORD of the universe is doing, who brings redemption and deliverance. This is where it connects with the joy that
is one of the seven characteristics of God's reign. As we noticed
in the previous chapter, verses 3 and 10 directly say the beatitudes
are about "the reign of God." The other beatitudes also celebrate
participation in God's coming reign: we will be comforted by

God, inherit the earth, be filled (with delivering justice), receive God's compassion, see God, be called children of God,
and have great reward in God. All these are rewards of participating in God's reign. This experience is already beginning in
Jesus.

BEYOND HIGH IDEALS

Many people have interpreted the beatitudes as high ideals that
Jesus is urging us to live up to. This is the ethics of *idealism,*
focusing attention on our own good works and hard effort rather than on participation in God's grace. It urges us to make a
superhuman effort to live up to ideals that are difficult if not
impossible to reach. It often leads people to praise Jesus for
teaching wonderfully high ideals, but then to say that in real life
we have to live by some other, more realistic ethic.

When seen as a type of idealism, Jesus' teachings are about
imposing an ethic (a set of principles, moral values, or ideals) on
us from above that does not fit our real struggle. They seem to
be foreign to our nature, like a pair of pants too tight for our
body, or a job that does not fit our gifts and interests. We try to
make our reality fit the ideals, but it simply does not fit. Idealistic thinking is wishful, not realistic. It does not point out the way
to deal with real problems.

The more we emphasize these teachings as ideals to live up
to, the guiltier and less worthy we feel. Some of us even avoid
Jesus' teachings. Or if we think we do live up to these ideals, we
become self-righteous. We thank God that we are not like other
people, who are not so virtuous as we are. Our moralistic arrogance makes us hard to live with.

All of this imposes a Greek philosophy of idealism on the real
Jewish Jesus, who identifies with the realistic tradition of the
Hebrew prophets, not the tradition of Greek idealism. The gospel
is about God coming to deliver us, not our building ourselves
up to attempt to reach God's heights by living out impossibly
high ideals.

THE BEATITUDES AND GOD'S GRACIOUS DELIVERANCE

One way to understand the difference between an idealistic interpretation of the beatitudes and what is really intended is to ask, Is Jesus saying "Joyful are those who are poor and humble before God" *because being poor and humbled makes them virtuous* so they will get the reward that virtuous people deserve? Or is he saying, "Joyful are those who are poor and humble before God" *because God is gracious and God is acting to deliver the poor and humble*? There is a huge difference in the two readings of this one beatitude—and it leads to an entirely different view of what God is doing in our lives.

Idealism speaks to people who are not what the ideals urge. It promises that if they live by the ideals they will get rewards. The beatitudes are not like that. They speak to disciples who already are being made participants in the presence of the Holy Spirit through Jesus Christ; we already know at least a taste of being saddened or criticized, being peacemakers, and so on. They do not promise distant well-being and success; they celebrate the reality that God is already acting to deliver us. They are based not on the perfection of the disciples but on the coming of God's grace, already experienced in Jesus (Matt. 13:31, 17:20; Mark 4:31; Luke 13:19).

One clue to seeing how Jesus intended these teachings is in how he based them on the same 61st chapter of Isaiah that he read when he gave his inaugural sermon in Luke 4:18:

> The Spirit of the Lord is upon me
> Because he has anointed me;
> He has sent me to bring good news to the poor,
> to proclaim release for the prisoners
> and recovery of sight for the blind;
> to let the broken victims go free,
> to proclaim the year of the Lord's favor.

Is this a passage about human effort to live up to high ideals? Is it urging us to become poor, prisoners, blind, and victims so that God will reward us? I don't think so. It is a passage of celebration because God is acting graciously to deliver us from our poverty and captivity into God's reign of deliverance, justice, and joy. Notice how Jesus was referring to this prophetic passage of deliverance when he taught the beatitudes:

Isaiah 61	Matthew 5
61:1 The Spirit of the Lord is upon me, because the Lord has anointed me to preach good news to the poor. ["To preach good news" is closely bound to the Kingdom of God]	5:3 Blessed are the poor in spirit, for theirs is the kingdom of heaven.
61:2 To comfort all who mourn.	5:4 Blessed are those who mourn, for they shall be comforted.
61:1, 7 To preach good news to the humble; they will inherit the earth.	5:5 Blessed are the humble, for they shall inherit the earth.
61:3, 8, 11 [All speak of "righteousness"]	5:6 Blessed are those who hunger and thirst for righteousness. . . .
61:1 To heal the brokenhearted.	5:8 Blessed are the pure in heart, for they will see God.
61:3, 8, 11 [All speak of righteousness]	5:10 Blessed are those who have been persecuted for . . . righteousness, for theirs is the kingdom of heaven.
61:10–11 Let my soul be glad in the Lord.	5:11–12 Blessed are you when people revile you. . . . Rejoice and be joyful, for your reward is great in heaven; for so persecuted people the prophets.[1]

The beatitudes are not about high ideals but about God's gracious deliverance and our joyous participation. Here in the Sermon on the Mount, Jesus says we are blessed because God is not distant and absent; we experience God's reign and presence in our midst and will experience it even more in the future. Therefore each beatitude begins and ends with the joy, the happiness, the blessedness of the good news of participation in God's gracious deliverance. The beatitudes say what Isaiah 35:3–4 says: "Strengthen the tired hands and revive the stumbling knees. Say to the despairing hearts: Be of good cheer. Do not be afraid. See, your God is coming."[2]

Once we understand the beatitudes prophetically as God's gracious deliverance, they match up well with the seven characteristics of the reign of God. They also match up with Jesus' characteristic teaching of the parables of the kingdom. That's what I want to show in this chapter.

The Poor and Humble

"Joyful are those who are poor and humble before God, for theirs is the reign of God."

In the usual translations, Luke 6:20 says "Blessed are you who are *poor,*" but Matthew says "Blessed are the *poor in spirit.*" Which did Jesus teach? The poor, or the poor in spirit?

Both. Jesus was quoting Isaiah 61:1 in the Hebrew Bible. The Hebrew word *anawim* combines both meanings. It means poor, oppressed by the rich and powerful, powerless, needy, humble, lowly, and pious.[3] Matthew and Luke translate this Hebrew word into Greek. Therefore, I have translated it "poor and humble before God." As biblical scholar Robert Guelich says: "*The poor* in Judaism referred to those in desperate need (socioeconomic element) whose helplessness drove them to a dependent relationship with God (religious element) for supplying their needs and vindication. Both elements are consistently present. . . . For Matthew, the *poor in spirit* are those who find themselves waiting, empty-handed, upon God alone for their hope and deliverance while beset with abuse and rejection by those in their own social and religious context."[4]

The poor are blessed not because they are morally perfect but because God especially wants to rescue the poor. God knows that people who have power often use that power to advance their own privileges, and to seek more power. The poor get pushed aside and dominated. If you are poor, just one illness, just one divorce, just one addiction, or just one job loss can keep you from paying your bills, get you evicted, and even make you homeless.

Many Old Testament passages show that God is deeply concerned for the poor and protects them (Exod. 22:25–27, 23:10–11; Lev. 19:9–10, 23:22; Deut. 15:7–11; 2 Sam. 22:28; Ps. 72:2, 4, 12; Isa. 26:6, 49:13, 66:2; Zeph. 3:12). Many passages show that the rich and powerful who abuse the poor will be judged (Pss. 7, 10, 35:10, 37:14–15; Amos 8:4; Isa. 3:14 and 15, 10:2, 32:7; Ezek. 16:49, 18:12, 22:29; cf. Jer. 22:16 and Zech. 7:10).[5]

Being humble is not calling attention to how lowly I am, but calling attention to God's grace (Matt. 5:16). It is giving myself over to God, surrendering myself to God. To really depend on God is what fits God's reign. In Isaiah, God says: "I live . . . with the one who is contrite and lowly in spirit, to revive the spirit of the lowly and to revive the heart of the contrite" (57:15). "This is the one I esteem: he who is humble and contrite in spirit, and trembles at my word" (66:2).[6]

Jesus fulfills Isaiah 61:1–2 in bringing good news to the poor (Luke 4:16–21, 7:22; Matt. 5:3ff, 11:5). He offers his presence to the social and religious outcasts, inviting them into community, feeding them, making them into disciples. This is grace-based deliverance. This beatitude points to the good news that Isaiah's prophetic celebration of God's justice as deliverance of the poor, oppressed, humble, needy, weak, and lowly is happening in Jesus the Messiah, and in the community practices of Jesus' followers. What greater meaning in life can there be than to participate, even in a little way, like a mustard seed, in the deliverance that God brings in Jesus?

Jesus teaches that the widow who gave two cents is the example of the breakthrough of the reign of God: "Beware of the scribes, who like to walk around in long robes, and to be greeted with respect in the marketplaces, and to have the best seats in the synagogues and places of honor at banquets. They devour widows' houses and for the sake of appearance say long prayers. They will receive the greater condemnation."

He sat down opposite the treasury and watched the crowd putting money into it. Many rich people put in large sums. A poor widow came and put in two small copper coins, which are worth a penny. Then he called the disciples and said to them, "Truly I tell you, this poor widow has put in more than all those who are contributing to the treasury. For all of them have contributed out of their abundance; but she out of her poverty has put in everything she had, all she had to live on" (Mark 12:38–44).

Those Who Are Saddened

"Joyful are those who are deeply saddened to the point of action, for they will be comforted."

The usual translation of this beatitude is "Blessed are those who mourn, for they shall be comforted." I follow Clarence Jordan's insightful interpretation: "A mourner is not necessarily one who weeps. He is one who expresses a deep concern. If the one about whom he is concerned dies, he might express his grief by crying; he might also do it by praying, or in some other way. Tears aren't essential to mourning, *but deep concern is.*"[7]

Clarence Jordan was a brilliant New Testament scholar best known for *The Cotton Patch Translation of the New Testament,* in which Galilee becomes his native South Georgia, Jerusalem becomes Atlanta, and the language is home-spun. He was deeply concerned about the sad state of economic conditions for poor farmers in South Georgia. He was also deeply concerned about the state of racial prejudice, segregation, and discrimination there. His undergraduate degree was in agriculture, and he believed he could make a difference teaching poor white and black farmers how to make a significantly better living. So instead of teaching the New Testament in a comfortable college or seminary, he became an agricultural missionary. He began a cooperative farm near Americus and Plains, Georgia, and enlisted whites and blacks to share in experimenting with crops and farming methods, developing a successful pecan-growing business. Those who farmed became co-owners, sharing work and proceeds as the early Christians did in the book of Acts (Acts 2:43–47, 4:32–37). They named the farm *Koinonia,* the New Testament Greek word for community, participation, sharing, or fellowship. They began sharing the gospel of Jesus Christ, in which there is repentance for racism, healing for the heritage of slavery and discrimination, and love for all neighbors. This was in 1942, twelve years before the *Brown* v. *Board of Education* Supreme Court decision that declared school segregation illegal and twenty years before the high point of the civil rights movement. It was astounding for Jordan to lead this effort in the most resistant part of Georgia, cotton plantation country. But he believed in the gospel. He believed in following Jesus.

The community at Koinonia was boycotted by the seed and feed store and had to develop its own marketing networks. They were shot at by drive-by racists. They were expelled from the local Southern Baptist church. But they survived and thrived; their witness spread far and wide. They are heroes for those Southern Baptists who are committed to the full gospel of Jesus Christ. Koinonia Farm still exists and still sells pecans. It has spawned Habitat for Humanity, which cooperatively builds homes and home ownership for poor families worldwide. It has inspired Christian commitment, in thousands of Southerners, to work to overcome racism, notably former president Jimmy Carter.

I will never forget what Clarence Jordan said when I heard him speak in 1958. Segregation is a dying horse. A dying horse may kick convulsively now and then. It can still do some damage to those who oppose it. But its time is over. It really is dying.

This was well before the rest of us discerned the truth he was telling us. But he saw the signs that we had not seen. Like a prophet of deliverance, he was using a vivid parable that called us to be participants in the fellowship of those who were bringing about the end of segregation. The task is not finished yet, and his call to have concern enough to work together in bringing about community is still powerful.

Jordan meant what he said when he defined *penthountes* (usually translated as mourning) as being deeply saddened and concerned to the point of action. He knew what he was saying, both because of his deep research in the Greek New Testament and because of his deep sharing in the way of Jesus. Because he lived the Sermon on the Mount, he could interpret it accurately. That too is a parable for us.

Penthountes does mean being sad because of a loss, as when your father dies or your sister is fired from her job. The reign of God will bring healing and comfort. But it also means *repentance*: Christians who pray for God's reign to come are all the more aware that what is happening in themselves and their society is far from God's reign. Their prayer life compares God's compassion for all people with the suffering, violence, injustice, and lack of caring that hurt people; they are realists as to the causes of the wrong. They truly want to end their sinning and serve God. They want to share in a community that experiences the mustard seeds of the kingdom, the small daily breakthroughs of God's reign.

The prophet Amos pronounces God's judgment on those who do not mourn: They oppress the poor and crush the needy and then say, "Bring something to drink!" They sin and then bring sacrifices to the temple, thinking their sacrifices cover their sins, even though they continue to practice injustice. God pronounces "Alas for those who are at ease in Zion. . . . Alas for those who . . . sing idle songs to the sound of the harp, . . . but are not grieved over the ruin of Joseph! . . . Surely I will never forget any of their deeds. Shall not the land tremble on this account, and everyone mourn who lives in it? . . . I will turn your feasts into mourning'" (Amos 4:1–5; 5:6, 14; 6:1–7; 8:7–10; 9:5). When Jesus calls for mourning, he means the mourning of repentance that is sincere enough to cause us to change our way of living.

Clarence Jordan writes: "There must be a concern about this bankrupt condition so deep that it will find some expression. We must be *really grieved* that things are as they are. Those people are not real mourners who say, 'Sure the world's in a mess, and I guess maybe I'm a bit guilty like everybody else, but what can I do about it?' What they're really saying is that they are not concerned enough about themselves or the world to *look* for anything to do. No great burden hangs on their hearts. They aren't grieved. They don't mourn."[8]

Now we see that this beatitude connects with Jesus' announcement of the coming of the reign of God ("*Repent,* for the reign of God is at hand"; Matt. 4:17). It also connects with Isaiah 61:2 ("to comfort those who mourn"; "The Lord God will wipe away the tears from every face, and death and mourning will end"; Isa. 25:8; Rev. 21:4).

Jesus teaches several parables about realistically recognizing the need to be concerned to the point of action. There is, for example, the parable of the son who at first told his father "I am not going to" but then "later felt remorse and went" (Matt. 21: 28–32). See also Luke 16:1–8 and Matthew 11:16–19.

Those Who Surrender to God

"Joyful are those whose wills are surrendered to God, for they will inherit the earth."

Here Jesus is quoting Psalm 37:11 (more on this in a moment), which uses the same Hebrew word for *humble* that we saw in Isaiah 61:1, quoted in the first beatitude. This beatitude has basically the same meaning: humble in the sense of surrendered to God, as well as socially and economically poor or powerless. If we are poor and surrendered to God, we are blessed, because in Christ God delivers us, and we shall inherit the earth.

Jordan says it would be better to translate the Greek word *praeis*, "completely surrendered to the will of God" rather than meek. It means their will has been tamed by God's will:

> In English, the word "meek" has come to be about the same as "weak" or "harmless" or "spiritless." It is thought that a meek person is something of a doormat upon which everyone wipes his feet, a timid soul who lives in mortal fear of offending his fellow creatures. But nothing could be more foreign to the biblical use of the word. It is used in particular to describe two persons: Moses (Num. 12:3) and Jesus (Matt. 11:29). One of them defied the might of Egypt and the other couldn't be cowed by a powerful Roman official. . . . Both of them seemed absolutely fearless in the face of men, and completely surrendered to the will of God. . . . People may be called [tamed] to the extent that they have surrendered their wills to God and learned to do his bidding. . . . They won't listen to any man, no matter what his power or influence, who tries to make them compromise or disobey their Master's voice. . . . They surrender their will to God so completely that God's will becomes their will. . . . They become God's "workhorses" on earth.[9]

There is another connotation as well. Wherever the Greek word *praeis* occurs in the Bible, it always points to peacefulness or peacemaking. Matthew 21:5 is a quote from Zechariah 9:9, where the entrance of the *nonviolent or peacemaking* Messianic king is described:

> Your king is coming to you,
> his cause won, his victory gained,
> *humble* and mounted on an ass,
> on a foal, the young of a she-ass.

He shall banish chariots from Ephraim
and war-horses from Jerusalem;
the warrior's bow shall be banished.
He shall speak peaceably to every nation,
and his reign shall extend from sea to sea,
from the River to the ends of the earth.

This peacemaking theme is clear also in Psalm 37:11. In fact, Psalm 37 (NIV) includes most of the characteristics of the reign of God:

4 Delight yourself in the LORD. . . .
6 He will make your righteousness shine like the dawn, the justice of your cause like the noonday sun. . . .
8 Refrain from anger and turn from wrath. . . .
9 Those who hope in the LORD will inherit the land. . . .
11 But the meek will inherit the land and enjoy great
        peace. . . .
14 The wicked draw the sword and bend the bow,
        to bring down the poor and needy,
        to slay those whose ways are upright.
29 The *righteous* will inherit the land,
        and dwell in it forever.
        The mouth of the *righteous* man utters wisdom,
        and his tongue speaks *what is just.*
37 There is a future for the man of *peace.* . . .
39 The salvation of the *righteous* comes from the Lord,
        He is their stronghold in time of trouble;
        the Lord helps them, and *delivers* them;
        He *delivers* them from the wicked
        and *saves* them.

The two meanings—humbly surrendered and peacemaking—fit together. Martin Luther King Jr. said, "Jesus understood the difficulty inherent in the act of loving one's enemy. . . . He realized that every genuine expression of love grows out of a consistent and total surrender to God."[10]

Jesus also taught a parable about not being surrendered to God and treating others with contempt instead of peace:

> Two men went up into the temple to pray, one a Pharisee and the other a tax collector. The Pharisee stood and prayed these things concerning himself: "God, I thank you that I am not like the rest of men—thieves, swindlers, adulterers, or even like this tax collector. I fast twice a week; I pay tithes on all that I acquire."
>
> But the tax collector, standing far off, would not even lift up his eyes to heaven, but beat his breast, saying, "God, be merciful to me a sinner!"
>
> I tell you, this man went down to his house justified rather than the other; for every one who exalts himself will be humbled, but he who humbles himself will be exalted [Luke 18:10–14].

Arland Hultgren, an expert in parables, comments: "The Pharisee implicitly considers himself an autonomous agent of moral virtue; he is hardly dependent upon God for anything. And if he is not dependent upon God, he has no reason to give thanks to God."[11] That superior attitude alienates him from persons he considers outcasts. His self-righteousness is the opposite of peacemaking.

Those Who Thirst for Justice

"Joyful are those who hunger and thirst for restorative justice, for they will be filled."

The key to this beatitude is to understand the meaning of righteousness, which I have translated as "restorative justice." What are we hungering and thirsting for when we hope and long for righteousness?

Like *meek,* the word *righteousness* does not communicate the meaning accurately. Because our culture is individualistic and possessive, we think of righteousness as the virtue that an individual person possesses. But this kind of righteousness is self-righteousness, and that is exactly what the gospel says we cannot have (Rom. 3).

The Greek word for righteousness, *dikaiosyne,* and its root, *dike,* have the connotation of justice. Furthermore, Jesus is quoting Isaiah 61, which rejoices three times that God is bringing righteousness or justice (verses 7, 10, and 11). (The word there is the Hebrew, *tsedaqah.*) Since Jesus quoted the Bible in Hebrew (or Aramaic), not in English or Greek, we need to ask what *tsedaqah* means in Isaiah and elsewhere in the Law and Prophets. As we saw in Chapter Two, it means delivering justice (justice that rescues and releases the oppressed) and community-restorative justice (justice that restores the powerless and the outcasts to their rightful place in covenant community). This is why it appears so often in the Hebrew Bible in parallel with the other word for justice, *mishpat* (see Ps. 37, quoted earlier, and Chapter Two). This is also why the hungry and the thirsty hunger and thirst for righteousness; they yearn bodily for the kind of justice that restores them to community where they can eat and drink. It may be that only those readers who have experienced injustice, hunger, and exclusion from community can fully experience the significance of what the Bible means by justice. But they are the kind of people who especially flock to Jesus.

It is no accident that in the Sermon on the Mount Jesus emphasizes giving to the one who begs; giving alms as service to God rather than for show; and not hoarding money for ourselves but giving it to God's kingdom and righteousness (Matt. 5:42, 6:2–4, 19–34).

Jesus taught a memorable parable about hungering and thirsting for delivering justice:

A rich man was clothed in purple and fine linen and feasted sumptuously day by day. And at his gate a poor man named Lazarus was laid, full of sores, who desired to be fed with what fell from the rich man's table. . . .

The poor man died and was carried by the angels to Abraham's bosom. The rich man also died, and he was buried; and in Hades, being in torment, he lifted up his eyes and saw Abraham far off and Lazarus in his bosom. And he called out, "Father Abraham, have mercy upon me, and send Lazarus to dip the end of his finger in water and cool my tongue; for I am in anguish in this flame." But Abraham said . . . no one may cross from there to here.

And he said, "Then I beg you father, to send him to my father's house, for I have five brothers, in order that he may warn them, lest they also come into this place of torment."

But Abraham said, "They have Moses and the prophets; let them hear them" [Luke 16:19–31].

Moses and the prophets and Jesus teach a different kind of justice from leaving the starving outside the gate, hungry.

Jesus teaches a kind of justice that focuses on deliverance from need. Most of us remember the parable of the workers who were hired at six in the morning, and others at nine, and others at noon, at three, and at five. The ones hired late had been standing all day without work, "because no one hired us." When evening came, the owner paid them all a denarius, which was a normal day's wage. The parable puzzles us, because we think of pay as getting what we deserve. But Jesus was thinking of what a worker needs to feed his family. He was thinking of the kind of justice that delivers unemployed workers from their need. Twice in the parable, the owner says he is doing what is just, not what is unjust (Matt. 20:4, 13). Jesus says the kingdom of heaven is like this (Matt. 20:1). As we saw in the previous chapter, the reign of God is characterized by delivering, restorative justice.

Those Who Practice Compassion in Action

"Joyful are those who practice compassion in action, for they will receive God's compassion."

The Greek word for "compassion in action" here, *eleémones,* usually translated "merciful," means generous in doing deeds of deliverance. Mercy is about a generous action that delivers someone from need or bondage. Clarence Jordan writes: "By 'the merciful' he means *those who have an attitude of such compassion toward all people that they want to share gladly all that they have with one another and with the world.*"[12] Mercy in the Gospels can mean forgiveness that delivers from the bondage of guilt, or (more often) healing or giving that delivers from the bondage of need. Jesus does not split forgiveness from deeds of mercy; they are all part of God's mercy. As Jesus walks down the road and a blind or crippled person calls out, "Have mercy on me," the person does not mean "Let me off easy" or "Forgive me" but "Heal me; deliver me from my affliction." This is why in Matthew 6:2 doing mercy, *eleémosynen,* means giving alms for the poor. (See also Matt. 18:33 and 23:23; cf. 12:7.)

Isaiah emphasized God's compassion as motivation for justice that particularly focuses on deliverance from need, and so does Jesus. There are many lists of acts of kindness in the Old Testament and Jewish literature, especially Isaiah 58:6–7, which mentions freeing the oppressed, giving bread to the hungry, providing hospitality to the homeless poor, and covering the naked.[13]

A strong international movement at the turn of the twenty-first century successfully persuaded rich nations to forgive many of the debts of the forty poorest nations, so long as those nations agreed to international controls on their spending such that debt relief brought economic betterment to their people. The debts were so great that the poor nations could never have paid them back. The movement was named "Jubilee 2000" after Jesus' teaching of Jubilee forgiveness of debts. Like

Jesus' parable, it combined forgiveness and economic debt. It was an action of compassion and deliverance.

Bob Riley, a conservative winner of the Friend of Taxpayers Award several years running, was elected governor of Alabama in 2002. He found that the tax code had not changed since 1901. He pointed out that "the richest Alabamians paid 3 percent of their income in taxes, and the poorest paid up to 12 percent." Out-of-state timber companies paid only $1.25 per acre in property taxes. Alabama was third from the bottom of all states in total taxes, and almost all of that came from sales taxes, which are paid in higher proportion by people who need to spend most of their income on basic needs. As journalist Bill McKibben wrote: "So Riley proposed a tax hike, partly to dig the state out of a fiscal crisis and partly to put more money into the state's school system, routinely ranked near the worst in the nation. He argued that it was Christian duty to look after the poor more carefully." The outcome would have been that the owner of a $250,000 home paid $1,432 in property taxes. But the leader of the Christian Coalition of Alabama spearheaded the opposition, saying, "You'll find most Alabamians have got a charitable heart. They just don't want it coming out of *their* pockets." (What does charity mean if it cannot come out of your own pocket? Maybe we need a new phrase, "greed-motivated charity"—aid to the poor that is not allowed to affect one's own pocketbook.) The law was defeated and the schools stayed underfunded. Governor Riley commented, "I'm tired of Alabama being first in things that are bad, and last in things that are good."[14]

Jesus taught a parable that combined forgiveness of sins and forgiveness of debts, as acts of mercy:

> A woman in the city, who was a sinner, having learned that he was eating in the Pharisee's house, brought an alabaster jar of ointment. She stood behind him at his feet, weeping, and began to bathe his feet with her tears and to dry them with her hair. Then she continued kissing his feet and anointing

them with the ointment. Now when the Pharisee who had invited him saw it, he said to himself, "If this man were a prophet, he would have known who and what kind of woman this is who is touching him—that she is a sinner."

Jesus spoke up and said to him . . . "A certain creditor had two debtors; one owed five hundred denarii, and the other fifty. When they could not pay, he canceled the debts for both of them. Now which of them will love him more?" Simon answered, "I suppose the one for whom he canceled the greater debt." And Jesus said to him, "You have judged rightly."

Then turning toward the woman, . . . he said to her, "Your sins are forgiven" (Luke 7:36–48 RSV).

Those Who Seek God's Will Holistically

"Joyful are those who seek God's will in all that they are and do, for they will see God."

This beatitude has often been thought to be about inner purity—as if Jesus criticized the Pharisees for being preoccupied with laws concerning forbidding certain foods and performing rituals correctly and focused instead on inner spiritual purity. But it is more accurate to say that he emphasized the unity of inward roots and outward fruits (Matt. 7:15–21). We can see this in Matthew 15:11 ("Not what food goes into a person's mouth makes the person unclean, but what words come out of that person's mouth make him or her unclean").

Greek idealism splits the inner soul from outward action. Biblical realism, by contrast, is holistic: there is one whole self in relation to one God, the Lord of all. Biblically, the heart is not our inner self but our relational organ. When I act angrily toward someone, my heart gets involved. It beats faster. The real split is not inner versus outer but serving God versus serving some other loyalty such as money or prestige. As biblical scholars W. D. Davies and Dale Allison point out, "Purity of heart must involve integrity, a correspondence between outward action and inward thought (cf. Matt. 15:8), a lack of duplicity, singleness of intention . . . and the desire to please God above all else. More succinctly: purity of heart is to will one thing, God's will, with all of one's being [and doing]."[15]

Integrity, which means the quality of being whole or undivided, is a state in which we are freed from our former masters (money, race prejudice, militarism, egotism, or any other of the jealous, demonic gods who demand our respect and obedience and make us their slaves). Jordan says that people's "conflicting loyalties make them wretched, confused, tense. And having to keep their eyes on two masters at once makes them cross-eyed, and their vision is so blurred that neither image is clear. But the eyes of the inwardly and outwardly pure are single, that is, focused upon one object, and their sight is not impaired. That's why Jesus said, 'for they shall see God.' They shall see God because their lives are in focus."[16] That is, their lives are in focus with the reign of God, which includes God's presence, as we saw in Isaiah.

Those Who Are Peacemakers

"Joyful are the peacemakers, for they will be called children of God."

Donald Hagner illuminates this beatitude with a reference to the historical and social context of the time: "In the context of the beatitudes, the point would seem to be directed against the Zealots, the Jewish revolutionaries who hoped through violence to bring the kingdom of God. Such means would have been a continual temptation for the downtrodden and oppressed who longed for the kingdom. The Zealots by their militarism hoped furthermore to demonstrate that they were the loyal 'sons of God.' But Jesus announces . . . it is the peacemakers who will be called the 'children of God.' . . . This stress on peace becomes a common motif in the New Testament (cf. Rom. 14:19; Heb. 12:14; James 3:18; 1 Pet. 3:11)."[17] It also fulfills what Isaiah prophesied: the reign of God brings *peace.*

Jesus' parable of the weeds and the wheat teaches that we are not to root out, exclude, or do violence against those in the Christian community, or outside it, who disagree with the gospel as we understand it. We should let both the weeds and the wheat grow together until the harvest (Matt. 13:24–30, 37–43).

This parable was central for those seventeenth-century Christians who developed religious liberty and independence of the church from the state; heretics should be allowed to live in peace. This ended the centuries-long practice of imprisoning and executing heretics. It was the key peacemaking development that ended the wars of religion.[18]

In Luke 15, three parables teach that we should not exclude outsiders but welcome them: the lost sheep, the lost coin, and the lost (Prodigal) son. All three are responses to the complaints of the Pharisees and Scribes that Jesus eats with tax collectors and sinners. Here Jesus fulfills the theme of Isaiah that the Holy One of Israel is the Redeemer, not the Separator. The lost coin portrays a woman as a metaphor for God. She has great *joy* when she finds it: "Just so, I tell you, there is joy in the presence of the angels of God over one sinner who repents" (Luke 15:9–10). The lost (Prodigal) son parable urges the elder brother to rejoice at his lost brother's return, not be hateful toward his brother. In fact, there is joy and rejoicing in Luke 15:5, 6, 7, 9, 10, 22–24, and 32. Jesus urges peacemaking with outsiders, the lost, and the heretics. Likewise, his parable of the compassionate Samaritan (Luke 10:25–37) urges peacemaking even with those who are a hated other.

Those Who Suffer and Are Persecuted

"Joyful are those who suffer because of restorative justice, for theirs is the reign of God."

"Joyful are you when they criticize, persecute, and slander you, because of me. Rejoice and be glad, for your reward is great in God. For in the same way they persecuted the prophets before you."

These two teachings are the climax of the beatitudes. They warn us realistically that the world is full of sin and will not always welcome our good news. Despite that, we work for the kind of delivering justice that God, in compassion for the persecuted and oppressed, works to bring about.

Dietrich Bonhoeffer wrote his classic book on the Sermon on the Mount, *The Cost of Discipleship,* just as Hitler was coming to power as dictator of Germany. Matthew 5:10 ("Joyful are those who suffer *because of restorative justice,* for theirs is the reign of God") gave Bonhoeffer a solid rock of justice to stand on against Hitler's injustice. Most German Christians were actually sucked into supporting Hitler. But Bonhoeffer's full commitment to following the way of Jesus gave him clarity and courage to speak out and lead other Christians in opposing Hitler's injustice and violence against Jews.

A few years later, when Bonhoeffer wrote his *Ethics,* struggling to define Christian responsibility in the midst of an unimaginably evil and dangerous dictatorship, this beatitude ("Joyful are those who suffer because of delivering justice, for theirs is the reign of God") was the one passage from the Sermon on the Mount that he decisively emphasized as giving the guidance we need. He pointed out that Jesus commended those who suffer because of their work for justice, not only those who do it in Jesus' name. God cares deeply and compassionately for justice for his creation, for all people, including Jews in German society; God blesses those who suffer in their work for justice. This teaching continued to give Bonhoeffer strong guidance amid horrible evil. It enabled him to stand, speak, and lead when others ducked, were silent, and were duped by the unjust ideology of powerful authoritarianism.[19]

Bonhoeffer was thoroughly Christ-centered in his ethics. Both his *Cost of Discipleship* and his *Ethics* strongly emphasized God's will as revealed in Jesus Christ. Those Christians who

were not taken in by Hitler's ideology usually had a strongly
Christ-centered ethic with a full and concrete understanding of
the way of Jesus and the Lordship of Christ over all of life, not
only over a "religious" part of life.[20] That is one of my main
motivations in writing this very book. I want all Christians to
have a concrete understanding of the way of Jesus so they will
stand on the rock when the winds of various ideologies blow us
to and fro.

Jesus' climax at the end of the beatitudes says exactly this:
stand faithful and do not get blown about by the ideologies of
the world. He taught that we are the salt of the earth, but if the
salt loses its saltiness it is good for nothing but to be thrown
onto the sand and trampled under foot (Matt. 5:13–16). Jesus is
talking about being different from the world, having a different
taste. If we lose our distinction from the world's greed, uncar-
ing, self-centeredness, exclusionism, unfaithfulness, and violence, then we have no purpose. We are tasteless and useless.
Here Jesus is probably praising the Qumran community that
moved down by the Dead Sea, which is so salty they could
evaporate the water and make table salt. They were indeed a
right salty community. They were definitely different from the
world and its compromises.

But Jesus also taught that we are the light shining in the
world. Nobody lights a lamp and then hides it away so people
cannot see it. The problem with the Qumran community was
they were hiding their witness. We are to be different from the
world, but we are to let the world see our light, pointing to the
way of God in the world.

Many people say we are to be *salt and light*. But this leaves
out the climax. We are to be salt, light, and *deeds*. Jesus' teaching
is threefold. The climax comes with the deeds. The one command in the teaching is to "*shine your light* before others so they
may see your good works and give glory to God."

Why do people often leave out the climax and say only "salt
and light"? Perhaps it is because they aren't doing the deeds.
Unless we are walking the talk, we are not authentic salt; we are

no different from the sand underfoot, nor are we a light that actually shines in the world. If we are not doing justice for Jesus' sake, the world has no reason to heed us, to allow us to disturb them. It is by our deeds that they see God's light and give God the glory—and maybe come to persecute us. It is by our deeds that they know we are different. The way people see God's light is not because we sing praise songs but because of our actions. Remember the story of Parush Parushev in Chapter One, who was converted from Communist atheist to faithful Christian when he saw how a community of Christians in Poland were living their faith. It is a parable for our time. Jesus' teaching is *salt, light, and deeds.*

> The kingdom of heaven is like a grain of mustard seed which a man took and sowed in his field; it is the smallest of all the seeds, but when it has grown it is the greatest of shrubs and becomes a tree, so that the birds of the air come and make nests in its branches [Matt. 13:31–32; see also Mark 4:30–32 and Luke 13:18–19].
>
> And again [Jesus] said, "to what shall I compare the kingdom of God? It is like leaven that a woman took and hid in three measures of flour, until it was all leavened" [Luke 13:20–21; see also Matt. 13:33].

The parable of the mustard seed is a truly important teaching of Jesus; all the Gospels include it. It is a life motto that I often repeat to myself: "Well, life isn't perfect, and I sure do have my limits, but every now and then a mustard seed sprouts, and thank God for the mustard seeds!" Or just for short, "Thank God for the mustard seeds!"

In Chapter Two we saw the characteristics of the breakthrough of God's reign in our midst: deliverance, God's presence, justice, peace, joy, healing, and return to God. But then some say, "But look around you: I see greed, injustice, violence, sickness, and people who are not returning to God but evading God's way right and left." Jesus' parable of the greedy and violent tenants says exactly that (Mark 12:1–12, Matt. 21:33, Luke 20:9–19). As Clarence Jordan reminds us, Jesus "was in truth the world's greatest realist."[21] But his parables of the patient farmer (Mark 4:26– 29), the mustard seed, and the leaven say that even in that realism the reign of God also breaks in here and there. The good news is we can be part of it. We can participate in what God is growing. Therefore we can have patience with realistic faith and hope that something good is growing here as well, among the weeds.

4

Practicing Reconciliation and Keeping Our Covenants

I n Matthew 5:21–48, Jesus gives us six teachings that realistically diagnose the vicious cycles, the repressed anger, the
broken relationships, the isolation, even the violence in
which we are stuck because of our captivity to self-defeating
habits or ways of domination. Then he shows how God is doing
something new in our lives: bringing God's way of deliverance
from these vicious cycles.

But Jesus' teachings have been badly misunderstood as if
they were high ideals and hard teachings. In this chapter, we
look at the first three of the teachings (Figure 4.1). Our purpose
is to see that they are a realistic way of deliverance from the
cycles of domination that Jesus diagnoses.

DEALING WITH ANGER

The idealistic interpretation has understood these teachings as
"antitheses"—composed first of a teaching from the Old Testament and second of Jesus' teaching "anti" the Old Testament. For
example, Matthew 5:21–26 is understood as: "You have heard
that it was said to those of ancient times, 'You shall not kill'; but
I say instead, do not even be angry." This, however, is not what
Jesus teaches. Instead, Jesus shows the way of deliverance from

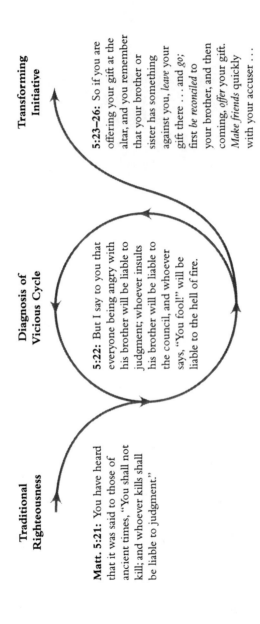

Traditional Righteousness

Matt. 5:21: You have heard that it was said to those of ancient times, "You shall not kill; and whoever kills shall be liable to judgment."

Diagnosis of Vicious Cycle

5:22: But I say to you that everyone being angry with his brother will be liable to judgment; whoever insults his brother will be liable to the council, and whoever says, "You fool!" will be liable to the hell of fire.

Transforming Initiative

5:23–26: So if you are offering your gift at the altar, and you remember that your brother or sister has something against you, *leave* your gift there . . . and *go*; first *be reconciled* to your brother, and then coming, *offer* your gift. *Make friends* quickly with your accuser . . .

Figure 4.1. Practices of Reconciliation.

vicious cycles of anger, disrespect, domination, and violence—
to transforming initiatives of peacemaking.

First, Jesus affirms a traditional teaching, from the Ten Commandments: "you shall not kill." Second, he diagnoses vicious
cycles of disrespect and domination that cause murder. Third, in
the climax, he shows the way of deliverance.

Traditional Righteousness:
The Commandment Against Murder

First Jesus calls our attention to the traditional teaching in the
Old Testament. In doing so, he supports the law in the Ten
Commandments that tells us not to murder, but he points us
toward prevention by noting the ingredients that lead us to do
violence to one another. Idealistic interpretations of this teaching usually say the Old Testament focuses on outer action while
Jesus corrects that by focusing on the inner attitude, on anger.
In this interpretation, Jesus' teaching is supposedly a command
never to be angry. But if we are honest, we know that it is impossible never to be angry. Jesus got angry many times—for example, at the hardness of heart of those who would not say it
was right to heal the man with the withered hand on the Sabbath (Mark 3:5). Matthew 21:12–17 and Matthew 23 show
Jesus angry. Additionally, in Matthew 23:17 Jesus calls his oppo-
nents fools, which would contradict 5:22 if that verse were a
command.

The Vicious Cycle: Anger and Judgment

The truth is that Jesus gave no command not to be angry. What
Jesus says here about anger is instead a diagnosis. It is a participle,
"being angry"—an ongoing action, continuing in anger; being
angry leads to judgment. We know in our own experience that
continuing to live in anger shows up in an ulcer, heart attack, bitterness, sometimes physical abuse, and even murder. Jesus wants us

to face the problem of anger realistically. Instead of commanding
us not to be angry, this teaching focuses on what we do with our
anger. Ephesians 4:26 says, "Be angry, but do not sin; do not let
the sun go down on your anger." The New Testament instructs
us to deal with our anger in a healing way that removes it.

A friend of mine was once a participant in a group discussion about anger. He said to the group, "I'm a Christian: I never
get angry." The group broke out in laughter, and he got furious
at them. He has now grown to the point where he laughs at
himself as he tells this story.

Jesus' teaching on anger is a realistic diagnosis of a vicious
cycle. If we are honest and realistic about ourselves, we know
that we all get angry now and then. We know that stewing in it,
continuing to live in anger, is a mechanism of temptation that
leads to alienation from God and neighbor, to a desire to insult
and dominate or even be violent, and therefore to destruction and
judgment. If Jesus commanded us never to be angry, that would
be a hard teaching, a high ideal, impossible to practice. Instead
he realistically diagnoses a vicious cycle that leads to judgment
and destruction. It is like a doctor's diagnosis of a tumor that will
lead to death if it is not removed.

The first murder in the Bible occurs in Genesis 4:3–7. It is
a story about the problem of Cain's anger at his brother, Abel—
anger that leads him to murder his brother. Cain is bringing his
sacrifice to the altar. In his anger at his brother, he wants *to dominate* him, *rise up above* him, and kill him (Gen. 4:8). God warns
Cain about the danger of remaining in anger and tells him he
can master it and do well.

In Matthew 5:21–26, Jesus also teaches about murder of a
brother. Just as in the story of Cain and Abel, he tells of a brother
bringing his sacrifice to the altar. Just as God warned Cain, Jesus
warns realistically about the danger that comes from remaining
in anger. He diagnoses the desire to rise up above the brother,
to insult him and call him fool. It's pretty clear that Jesus is
teaching realistically about the basic human experience por-
trayed in the original story of Cain and Abel. Jesus goes one step

farther: he tells us what it means to master the anger and do well (go talk with your brother and make peace).

Jesus now tells us what God means when God says to "do well" and "master it." It means to go find your brother, talk things over with him, and make peace: "Go, first be reconciled with your brother (or sister), and then come and offer your gift." This is the climax of the teaching: go make peace. This is Jesus' emphasis—the way of deliverance from the destructive consequences of anger.

In Cain and Abel's day, people got crops to grow by making a sacrifice to God, and hoping God would have regard for their sacrifice so the crops would grow. If their crops were not growing well, they said, "God had no regard for my offering." Cain thought his crops were not growing well because God did not like his sacrifice. If Cain had gone to his brother Abel, who was a successful farmer, Abel probably would have helped him be a better farmer. Then Cain would have had an alternative to staying stuck in the powerlessness of being angry and trying to farm without knowing how. It could have solved three relationship problems: with his brother, with God, and with his crops.

If there was anything wrong with his offering, it was that he was unwilling to go and make peace with his brother. God's way of deliverance includes peacemaking, as we saw when we studied the characteristics of the reign of God.

Maybe this is what Jesus means when he says we should make peace *before* we worship. (Paul makes the same point in 1 Cor. 11:18–20). Anger combined with unwillingness to make peace interferes with our relations with our brother or sister, and with God.

Transformation and Deliverance from Anger

The climax of Jesus' teaching is to go find the brother (or sister), talk things over, and try to make peace. It is not a command never to be angry. There are lots of signs that this is the main emphasis of Jesus' teaching:

- The climax has five commands in the Greek: *leave* your gift there, and *go*; first *be reconciled* to your brother, and then *offer* your gift. *Make friends* quickly. By contrast, the vicious cycle (the second part of the teaching) has no commands.
- In a biblical teaching with three parts (a triad), the third part is the climax.
- The climax has eighty-four words in the Greek. The vicious cycle has only thirty-nine.
- In the climax, Jesus goes one step farther than the story of Cain and Abel, telling us what God means by "you can do well; you can master it." It means, "you can go and make peace."
- Going to make peace with your brother is exactly what God does for us in Jesus Christ. God has reason to be angry with us but does not stay distant; God comes to us in Jesus and makes peace with us. This is what the reign of God is about. This is what grace means, what God does for us in Jesus. Going to make peace with the person we are angry with participates in God's grace, in God's loving way of deliverance.

We now see clearly that Jesus' teaching is a realistic way to face the problem of anger and domination. It moves from the powerlessness of being stuck in anger toward the empowerment of participating in God's way of grace and new life. Most of us have had the experience of being angry in a relationship, then talking with the other person, and resolving the problem. A person who was a source of anger becomes a friend. Our own sense of frustration and powerlessness is decreased. Sometimes it even turns toward cooperation and mutual support.

Andrew Lester is professor of pastoral theology and pastoral counseling in Brite Divinity School at Texas Christian University. He has spent a lifetime helping people deal constructively with their anger. He wrote *Coping with Your Anger*, which helped me personally cope with some of my own. He has now written *The Angry Christian*.[1] The first half of the book is devoted to showing realistically why we get angry. He works to help us overcome the tradition of idealism that causes us to deny our own anger. He shows various passages in the New Testament where Jesus is angry: at hardness of heart, at the disciples hindering people from bringing the children to him, at the money changers and sellers of animals who had taken over the place where Gentiles should be welcomed to the temple. Lester comments: "The fury of his words and the obvious force of his physical presence were burned into the disciples' minds. . . . Can anyone read this account [of the money changers in the temple] and doubt that Jesus was angry?" He encourages us to ask ourselves, "What emotions might we experience if we were present to hear" Jesus' words?[2]

Additionally, numerous passages in the Bible speak of God's anger. Again, Lester: "Scripture is clear that God becomes particularly angry in response to injustice against the helpless: widows, orphans, and other needy and oppressed persons. So when humans relate to other humans in ways that are abusive, oppressive, and painful, then God's fully invested and committed love is threatened, and God gets angry."[3] The point is that God's anger is rooted in God's love, especially God's love for the powerless.

The key step is to work on figuring out why we are angry. Anger is a useful diagnostic tool. It signals to us that something is wrong. It is a sixth sense for sniffing out wrong in our community. Just as Jesus teaches us to diagnose our vicious cycles realistically, anger alerts us to the need for some diagnosing. When Cain got angry, the first thing that God asked him was, "Why are you angry?" We need to hear the question from God as a helpful invitation to take responsibility for what is happening, particularly the interpretation we use to try to understand what is happening.

Lester recommends following Jesus' steps in Matthew 18: 15–17. Jesus says if a church member sins against you, go and talk it over when the two of you are alone. If the member listens to you, you may regain a friend. But if not, take one or two others along so that together you can try to work it out. If this does not work, then tell it to the church (which would have been a small house church, most likely), to see if the larger group can help achieve a reconciliation.

Jesus knew what harm could be done by unresolved anger. Therefore he instructs the disciples to take the initiative in seeking reconciliation with those whom we are angry at. If this individual initiative does not work, we should ask one or two people to accompany us in facilitating communication. As counselors well know, another person or two being present often allows a narrative to be expressed more fully and be heard. With one or two witnesses, accountability seems to increase. If this approach does not work, then a small group consultation or confrontation may be the next step. Here representatives of the community of faith try to mediate the dispute.[4]

I have seen in my own Sunday school class why it is important to carry out these steps in Jesus' order: do not take it before the whole group before individual initiative has done what it can to work out the problem first. If individual work is not done first, too much resistance and defensiveness in the presence of the whole group is likely to block the process. Again, we see the great wisdom of Jesus' way of deliverance.

As Jesus indicates by his comments on insult and put-down, we need to be aware of issues of power and the wish to dominate. Sometimes the person we are angry with is too sick, old, or powerless, or even no longer alive (as when it is anger with an elderly parent). Instead of confronting the person, we can find a trusted friend or counselor to help us work out the anger. We may find some outlet by writing a journal entry, or a letter that we do not send. This may also be true when the object of our anger has too much power over us such that it is unwise to express anger directly. Find a wise person to share it with. Surely this is advisable when the object of anger is a child. As a parent of three sons, I have slowly learned that it is wise to take time to cool down before expressing anger or punishment.

DEALING WITH SEXUAL TEMPTATION AND LUST

The next major teaching (Matt. 5:27–30) deals with the vicious cycle of sexual temptation, abuse, and harassment. Like anger, this too is a widespread experience, if we are honest. Again Jesus suggests we turn toward a way of deliverance, though he dramatizes it with some shock value so we will remember it.

First Jesus affirms a traditional teaching from the Ten Commandments, "you shall not commit adultery." Second he realistically confronts the vicious cycles that cause adultery. Third, he dramatizes the way of deliverance (Figure 4.2).

Traditional Righteousness: Adultery and Desire

As with anger, some have claimed that here Jesus criticizes the Old Testament or the rabbis of his time for focusing on outer action, whereas Jesus actually focuses on inner attitudes. But the Old Testament does not simply teach about outer action. Jesus is quoting commandments about *inner desires* of *coveting* "your neighbor's wife" as well as *outward actions* of adultery (Exod. 20:17). Jesus quotes the Old Testament when he says the main commandment is, "Hear, O Israel: the Lord your God, the Lord is one; you shall love the Lord your God with all your heart, and with all your soul, and with all your mind, and with all your strength." Elsewhere, he says, "You shall love your neighbor as yourself" (Mark 12:29–31). The Old Testament is concerned about the whole self, love and deeds.

The rabbis who taught at about the time of Jesus also taught against looking with lust in your eye as well as against actions of adultery, just as Jesus did. For example, the Testament of Issachar says, "I have not had intercourse with any woman other than my wife, nor was I promiscuous by lustful look." Rabbi Simeon ben Lakish said, "Even he who visualizes himself in the act of adultery is called an adulterer."

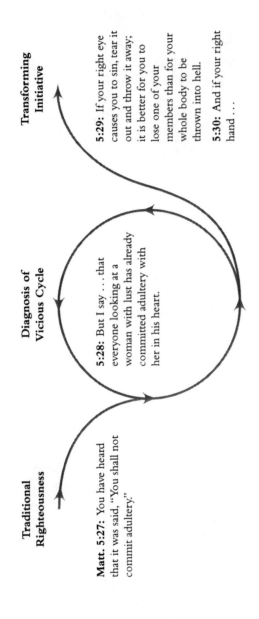

Transforming Initiative

5:29: If your right eye causes you to sin, tear it out and throw it away; it is better for you to lose one of your members than for your whole body to be thrown into hell.

5:30: And if your right hand . . .

Diagnosis of Vicious Cycle

5:28: But I say . . . that everyone looking at a woman with lust has already committed adultery with her in his heart.

Traditional Righteousness

Matt. 5:27: You have heard that it was said, "You shall not commit adultery."

Figure 4.2. Removing Lust-Creating Practices.

Jesus contradicts neither the Old Testament nor the Rabbis. He came "not to abolish" the law and the prophets "but to fulfill" them (Matt. 5:17). He focuses on the whole of life—actions and attitudes, doing and being. In his other teachings in the Sermon on the Mount, he also talks about actions: calling your brother a fool, divorcing, swearing oaths, praying in public for show, hoarding money, judging others. These are certainly about what we do, not just about attitude. For Jesus, it is the one who hears the teachings *and does them* who builds his or her house of faith on a solid foundation (Matt. 7:24). It is not the one who hears these words and *has a good attitude* toward them. Jesus does not separate being from doing; what we do shows who we are (Matt. 7:19–20).

The Vicious Cycle: Seeking to Possess

Likewise, in this teaching Jesus does not restrict himself to the inward desire. We are created with desires; desires come naturally. Jesus does not say, "Everyone who has a momentary flash of lust in his mind," but "everyone *looking with an aim to desire her.*" "Looking" is an action, an ongoing practice, like being angry and insulting someone else. He diagnoses looking with lust as a desire to possess, an intention to dominate, which then inflames the coveting desire. New Testament scholar Dale Allison says: "Luther got it right: 'It is impossible to keep the devil from shooting evil thoughts and lusts into your heart. But see to it that you do not let such arrows stick there and take root, but tear them out and throw them away.'"[5]

Looking with lust does not mean merely appreciating beauty. A normal man appreciates the beauty of women, as a normal woman appreciates attractive men. So does God: after God created man and woman in his image, he looked at them and celebrated: "God saw everything that he had made, and indeed, it was very good" (Gen. 1:31).

Pornography is one example of looking with lust. It is a $10 billion industry in the United States. A large number of scientific studies show that it influences viewers to associate sex with domination of women, including violence against them, rather than love and mutual covenant, and increasingly to accept that as OK. It portrays women as tied up, beaten, raped, humiliated, and even enjoying all this (after they initially resist). It influences viewers to be more likely to commit rape and murder. Almost every mass killer is found to have piles of pornography at home. Pornography does enormous harm to those who view it and to the persons they relate to afterward. Furthermore, it grows in appeal, as other addictions do. The best way to deal with it is to avoid any exposure, and tear it out if it is already happening. Sometimes people need counseling and help from a group to cure the addiction. Another way to deal with it is to pass laws prosecuting the perpetrators when it leads to harming people, as Canada has done—not just as obscenity, but as real harm to real people.

Transformation and Deliverance: Responsibility and Respect

When Jesus says the way of deliverance is to tear out the right eye and throw it away, he is being dramatic for shock effect. New Testament scholars agree that this is hyperbole, exaggeration to make an impression that will be remembered. Jesus' teaching has surely been remembered!

If I take the teaching literally and deal with lustful desire by tearing out my right eye, it will hardly solve the problem. I could wear a patch and still go on looking lustfully with my left eye. This teaching means we need to take radical action to remove the cause of the temptation. I should take the initiative to get rid of the practice that causes the lust—leering while imagining sexual possession, touching with lust in mind, meeting surreptitiously, treating women as sex objects. If I am a married man and enjoy lustful desires whenever I meet for lunch or private conversation with a woman who is not my wife, then I should quit meeting privately with her. If I need to meet because of the requirements of business, then we can bring someone else along.

If I meet her in my office, I can do so when my secretary is in. Or talk with a trusted Christian friend regularly and honestly about what I am doing. Men and women who proudly think they are above temptation are often the most likely to fall.

Notice that Jesus is putting the responsibility on the man. In Jesus' culture, women were usually blamed when men developed lustful relationships; a prominent example is the woman caught in adultery about to be stoned to death, in John 8:3–11. If she was caught in adultery, the man must have been caught too. Where was he when the stoning was about to happen?

In Jesus' time, rabbis were increasingly avoiding women and excluding them from public life.[6] Likewise, some cultures have strict requirements about how women must cover themselves, and how they should only walk behind a man, never in front of him where he is tempted to look at her. They label negatively women who engage in adultery but fail to do so with men. Jesus corrected that. He placed responsibility squarely on men for their actions, their habits, their practices. Men need to step up, take responsibility for their actions, and change those practices that lead to looking with lustful desire to possess. New Testament scholars Robert Guelich and Amy-Jill Levine comment that "one can meet the requirements of this demand only by means of a new relationship between men and women . . . no one should be regarded as a sex object."[7]

Jesus' teaching here is also found in Mark 9:42–7. Mark concludes the teaching: "Have salt in yourselves, and be at peace with one another." To have salt in ourselves means to be different from the ways of the world. To be at peace happens when men and women treat each other with respect and avoid practices that lead to adultery. Jesus is speaking with realism and wisdom.

COVENANT AND DIVORCE

Jesus also speaks realistically about divorce: it is usually tragic and complicated, even when it is the sad response to a greater tragedy.

I have friends who have gone through the confusing pain of anger, guilt, mutual abandonment, hurt, and the complex process of trying to reconstruct a new life without repeating the pattern of mistakes that led to that first deep disappointment. Probably you have too; you may even have experienced it yourself, or have experienced it in your own parents.

Jesus' teaching starts out looking like the same pattern that we have come to expect (see Figure 4.3).

Traditional Righteousness: Legalistic Divorce

The teaching on divorce (5:31–32) begins with a traditional teaching, just as we expect. Moses taught in Deuteronomy 24:1–4 that if a man divorces his wife, he gives her a certificate of divorce. Then she may become another man's wife.

The Vicious Cycle: Ruptured Relationships

Then comes the diagnosis of a vicious cycle, just as we expect. Divorcing causes adultery. If you have seen close friends divorce, or experienced divorce yourself, even if you thought it necessary or justified, you know it entails significant hurt and suffering, especially if children are involved. I interpret a little later what Jesus means in saying that it causes adultery, but we all know that suffering, hurt, and tragedy are involved.

Transformation and Deliverance: Reconciliation and Covenant Keeping

But surprisingly, there is no transforming initiative. We shall see as we study all fourteen teachings from Matthew 5:21 through 7:12 that Jesus always teaches a transforming initiative, a way of deliverance. But in this one teaching, it is missing. We are not told what initiative to take in hope of being delivered from the vicious cycle of divorcing. How can we explain this omission?

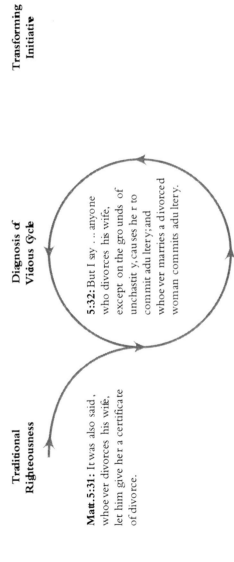

Traditional
Righteousness

Matt. 5:31: It was also said, whoever divorces his wife, let him give her a certificate of divorce.

Diagnosis of
Vicious Cycle

5:32: But I say ... anyone who divorces his wife, except on the grounds of unchastity, causes her to commit adultery; and whoever marries a divorced woman commits adultery.

Transforming
Initiative

Figure 4.3. Practices of Reconciliation in Marriage.

When I first began teaching the threefold pattern (or triads) of the Sermon on the Mount, I would say "the empty place in this teaching where a transforming initiative should be is so glaring that surely Jesus must have taught a transforming initiative something like Matthew 5:24 ('Go, be reconciled to your wife')." My students laughed at my audacity, thinking I could suggest what Jesus must have taught but that Matthew did not know to put it here where it belongs. I laughed too. But three years later I was working through 1 Corinthians and came upon 7:10–11. There Paul says "to the married I give this command— not I but the Lord. . . ." It comes, says Paul, from the Lord—a teaching of Jesus. Then Paul names the vicious cycle of divorcing twice, as Matthew 5:32 names divorcing twice. Finally Paul gives the command, an imperative, "be reconciled"! Just what I expected! Now I can say that I have the last laugh.

In its concluding verse, the Gospel of John says it could not include everything that Jesus did. We surely do not have all of Jesus' teachings. Paul wrote 1 Corinthians about thirty years earlier than the Gospel of Matthew was written, so it makes sense that he would have a teaching of Jesus that Matthew lacked. Matthew wrote carefully and faithfully. He did not make up teachings to fill in blank space.

Paul is surely right: the Lord, Jesus, taught that if we are considering a divorce we should try to make peace, try to work out reconciliation. Like the other teachings, it is stated as a command, an imperative in the Greek. The emphasis is not on legalistic arguments about when a divorce is or is not (tragically) necessary or justified. The emphasis is on ways to make peace.

David Gushee, who has written profoundly about marriage, offers wise and realistic guidance on how to heal a marriage and prevent divorce.[8] He does not think we should interpret Jesus legalistically. Paul did not; he allowed divorce not only in the case of sexual unfaithfulness (as in Matt. 5:32) but also in the case of a spouse not being a believer and separating (1 Cor. 7:15).

The covenantal structure of marriage is so binding that *only a fundamental and irreparable breach of the marriage covenant* can morally justify divorce. . . . As for remarriage, here the history of legalism has had devastating consequences. . . . Close reading of Paul's treatment of divorce in 1 Corinthians 7 helps us see that Jesus did not intend to bar all remarriage or classify all remarried persons as adulterers. He did intend to stop his hearers from finding false comfort in legal procedures that enable covenant breaking. . . . A pattern of physical and emotional abuse, the steady refusal of conjugal relations, the willful mistreatment or abuse of the couple's children, the refusal to contribute any effort to shared family labors either paid or unpaid, and the creation of an environment of unremitting hostility or hatred are all examples of violations of the covenant promises made on the wedding day. The circumstances in which such promise-breaking could create sufficient suffering to morally justify divorce cannot be determined by way of a general statement, but such circumstances exist."[9]

This fits what we see throughout the Sermon on the Mount: Jesus' emphasis is not on legalistic prohibitions but on transforming initiatives that deliver us from the vicious cycles.

How do you reconcile and make peace with your spouse? Gushee gives much wise advice, far more than I can summarize here. One key is communicating true feelings with each other instead of verbal withdrawal, put-downs, or dishonesty. This requires trustworthiness rather than dishonesty and therefore necessitates growth in character. Dishonesty often comes from the desire to evade discovery of unwelcome truth about oneself. Jesus' teaching about taking the log out of one's own eye is important guidance—we need to look for help in understanding where we are not seeing what is happening. A spouse can help day by day in that seeing; sometimes it is wise to ask a trained counselor to help us see what we are not seeing.

Marriage also requires mutual respect. The New Testament encourages us to practice speaking in a way that builds up rather than tearing down (Eph. 4:29–32). Insults and put-downs are what Jesus warns us about in Matthew 5:22. Peacemaking requires humility, willingness to repent and learn, eagerness to take the first step in initiating peace, practices of mercy and forgiveness, and desire to seek mutual agreement about what changes can satisfy both persons' need for justice and mutual respect.

Gushee also advocates a much deeper understanding of sex and marriage than simply expression of affection; rather, they are the meeting of basic creation relationships and basic needs for covenant faithfulness. This is like the theme that runs through both teachings of Jesus, on lust and divorce. Both of them diagnose the vicious cycle in terms of adultery. Why?

Jesus is deeply concerned about the intimate, created covenant relation between man and woman, and the vicious cycles that break the covenant relation. Jesus says we are created for faithful loyalty between us.

In the Bible, adultery is not only sexual behavior; the emphasis is on rupture of a covenant relationship—for example, violation of a marriage relationship.

Jesus says if I look at a woman as an object of my sexual desire to possess her I am already committing adultery with her in my heart. How can this be? It means that *I relate to her* in a way that breaks a covenant relation. First, I am being unfaithful to my covenant relation with my own wife, if I am married. How I relate to the other woman is unfaithful to her covenant with her husband, even if she is not aware of how I look at her. If neither of us is married, I treat her as an object of lust, a sex object, an object of my domination, and thus act unfaithfully to my covenant with her as a person created in the image of God, to whom I owe respect as a whole person.

In Matthew 19:4–6, Jesus quotes God's initial creation in Genesis: "For this reason a man shall leave his father and mother and be joined to his wife, and the two shall become one flesh."

Jesus emphasizes this deep, bodily covenant that they make, so deep that they actually become one: "So they are no longer two, but one flesh. Therefore what God has joined together, let no one separate."

Anyone who has entered into such a relation with another person—in marriage or even without marriage—knows that even if they later separate or divorce and go in their own direction, they are still part of one another. Frequent flashbacks of memory occur—of events marked by deep connection, deep insight, and, yes, deep hurt. There is also ongoing memory of what the other person said, appreciated, criticized, or wanted changed. There is a changed sense of who I am and how I have changed because of the influence of the other person. There is deep memory of how I acted toward the other, and of what this means for the person I want to be as I relate to others. If I have some spiritual sense, there is awareness that the way the other person and I relate also involves a deeper meaning and relationship, a fundamental meaning of life, an implicit even if not fully articulate relation to God, who cares about how I relate to others.

Jesus knew that we are created for deep intimacy and trust, for covenant relationships that require respect, trust, and faithfulness. This is why he shifted the question from Moses' teaching about divorce to the Genesis account of how we are created for one another. People who are not married also know the need and the yearning for friends who are loyal and faithful, who will speak the truth and can be counted on to care about them when they need caring for.

This is why Jesus puts such strong emphasis on being faithful and not manipulative in the way we look at each other as well as how we marry, and everything in between. Jesus is so much wiser than a culture that just focuses on self-advancement and neglects covenant relationships with one another.

5

Telling the Truth,
Making Peace,
Loving Our Enemies

When Yugoslavia split into Serbia, Bosnia, Croatia, Slovenia, and Kosovo, most of the Yugoslavian army had been Serbian soldiers so Serbia ended up controlling most of the military might. Possession of overwhelming offensive weapons is often a temptation, as it was for the Serbian dictator, Slobodan Milosevic. He made war first against Muslim Bosnia, then Catholic Croatia, and finally Muslim Kosovo. He combined his own demagogic drive for power with Serbian nationalism and Russian Orthodox loyalties. He made the words "ethnic cleansing" infamous in our vocabulary, as Serbian troops drove people of other ethnic groups and religions out of their homes, raping and massacring as they went, while they themselves held up three fingers in a symbol for the Trinity. The world responded in revulsion, and Serbian troops were driven out of all three countries. Serbs then threw Milosevic out of power in a democratic election. But the outcome was the bitterness that follows war, especially war that sets ethnic groups mixed with religion against each other. Milosevic was undergoing trial in international court in the Hague for war crimes when he died.

TELLING THE TRUTH

Vicious cycles like war and violence, dishonesty and manipulation, are what Jesus is diagnosing realistically in the Sermon on the Mount. And he shows how God is doing something new in our lives: bringing God's way of deliverance from these vicious cycles.

This is, once again, not a matter of high ideals and hard teachings but of transformation and deliverance. In a time of nuclear, chemical, and biological weapons; terrorism; civil war; and ethnic cleansing, followers of Jesus have a gospel that the world badly needs. We can receive and spread his gospel with joy. See Figure 5.1.

Traditional Righteousness: False and True Vows

Jesus may be pointing us to the Ten Commandments in Matthew 5:33–37 as well: "You shall not make wrongful use of the name of the LORD your God, for the LORD will not acquit anyone who misuses his name" (Exod. 20:7). The Old Testament clearly teaches against swearing falsely (Lev. 19:12; Num. 30:2; Deut. 23:21–23; Zech. 8:17). Ecclesiastes 5:5 says pretty much what Jesus says: "It is better that you should not vow than that you should vow and not fulfill it."

The Vicious Cycle: False Claims and Oaths

Jesus is concerned about both truthfulness and God's holy name. Each kind of swearing uses loyalty to God to manipulate and dominate another person through false claims. What a wrongful use of the name of God!

Matthew 23:16–22 shows the kind of vicious cycle that Jesus is concerned with. He says, "Woe to you, blind guides, who say, 'Whoever swears by the sanctuary is bound by nothing, but

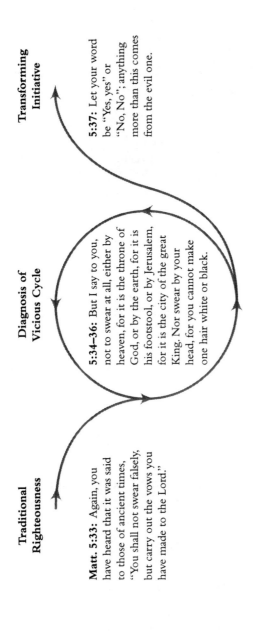

Traditional
Righteousness

Matt. 5:33: Again, you
have heard that it was said
to those of ancient times,
"You shall not swear falsely,
but carry out the vows you
have made to the Lord."

Diagnosis of
Vicious Cycle

5:34-36: But I say to you,
not to swear at all, either by
heaven, for it is the throne of
God, or by the earth, for it is
his footstool, or by Jerusalem,
for it is the city of the great
King. Nor swear by your
head, for you cannot make
one hair white or black.

Transforming
Initiative

5:37: Let your word
be "Yes, yes," or
"No, No"; anything
more than this comes
from the evil one.

Figure 5.1. Practices of Truth Telling.

whoever swears by the gold of the sanctuary is bound by the oath.' You blind fools! For which is greater, the gold or the sanctuary that has made the gold sacred?"

Here the practice makes an oath that sounds real (swearing by the sanctuary) but actually has a cross-your-fingers-behind-your-back secret limitation that you are not really committed to do what you promise to do. This is first of all untruthful. But more, you are taking advantage of a person, trying to manipulate and dominate him or her by deceit. Third, it is using *God's sanctuary* to deceive and manipulate, which is a horrendous betrayal of God's care for justice for the powerless and vulnerable.

We also notice that Jesus is angry here, calling the blind guides "fools." This supports what we saw in the last chapter: Jesus did not legalistically command people never to be angry, and not even never to call anyone a fool, but commanded that when we are angry we need to talk directly and explain what is wrong so we can make peace. Here his "talk" is a direct confrontation. Jesus' love includes the kind of tough love that confronts directly when necessary. It names the vicious cycle realistically.

Jesus continues: "And you say, 'whoever swears by the altar is bound by nothing, but whoever swears by the gift that is on the altar is bound by the oath.' How blind you are! For which is greater, the gift or the altar that makes the gift sacred? So whoever swears by the altar, swears by it and by everything on it, and whoever swears by the sanctuary, swears by it *and by the one who dwells in it*; and whoever swears by heaven, swears by the throne of God and *the one who is seated upon it*."

Notice the words in italics: they emphasize the presence of God. Jesus focuses on God's presence—one of the seven characteristics of the reign of God. Whenever we make a promise or say anything to someone else, and certainly whenever we take an oath, we do it in God's presence. If we claim to be followers of Jesus, we represent his presence to others. Therefore, making a false promise or speaking an untruth is doing it in God's presence, and making a negative testimony to Jesus.

Here is a clue for what Jesus means by going beyond the righteousness of the Pharisees (Matt. 5:20). It means being more truthful, and in particular it means serving God first, above other loyalties.

Transformation and Deliverance

Some followers of Jesus have refused ever to swear an oath. Historically, the Quakers were faced with sentences for contempt of court when they refused. But they earned an outstanding reputation for telling the truth. Eventually they won court provisions to allow Quakers to affirm the truth of what they were saying and avoid taking oaths. Their reputation for telling the truth fits the main point of this passage: it is more about being truthful to other persons in God's presence than about oaths. (We are always in God's presence.)

The command, the imperative, in Jesus' teaching is "*Let your word be* 'Yes, Yes' or 'No, No.'" His emphasis is on the way of deliverance: being truthful. In Jesus' society, saying the words twice (yes, yes) intensified the meaning—saying yes and really meaning yes, a true yes.

Learning to tell the truth begins in early childhood. Babies bond with their parent(s) from early on, and the quality of their communication is crucial. I still remember clearly the impression my mother made on me when she said she would always know if I was telling the truth.

As a young boy I would go to the farmer's market with my grandfather, a German immigrant tomato farmer. His bushels of tomatoes were beautiful, all on display! One day a customer came by and began lifting out the top tomatoes to see if those on the bottom were as good as those on the top. I remember what my grandfather said in his deep, gruff voice and heavy German accent: "Dey're da same t'rough an t'rough; ya don't believe it, ya go buy somewhere else!" Though the customer would have heard that as "true and true," he meant "through and through"—all the way through. My grandpa was so honest that he was offended if someone even hinted he might be deceiving customers about the quality of his tomatoes. His honesty was so widely known that he could afford to chase away the rare customer who might doubt him. In fact, his reputation was so sterling that the town of West St. Paul, Minnesota, elected my grandpa—with his sixth-grade education, German accent, and modest means—mayor of the town. For the rest of my life, his deep, gruff voice has been echoing in my head: "True and true, through and through." He is my model for being truthful, all the way through.

Today's corporate culture, often emphasizing profits as the one goal that counts, and today's political culture, often using information not as respect for truth but as what's effective in tearing down the reputation of a rival, threaten the quality of truth in our society. Yet when a corporation is shown to be untruthful, we see it heavily penalized and even driven into bankruptcy. When people lose confidence in the veracity of a president—as happened to Lyndon Johnson over the Vietnam War, Richard Nixon over Watergate, Bill Clinton over personal matters, and George W. Bush over claims of weapons of mass destruction in Iraq despite United Nations inspection reports to the contrary—it gradually eroded their popular support. By contrast, presidents of both parties who cultivated greater respect for the truth—notably Harry Truman, Dwight Eisenhower, Jimmy Carter, and Gerald Ford—grew in stature and respect. We should not become cynical and give up on demanding truth from our leaders. Our leaders set much of the moral tone for the nation.

The theological ethicist Dietrich Bonhoeffer faced a major challenge to truthfulness during the Nazi regime in Germany in World War II. Bonhoeffer was involved in a secret project that successfully helped Jews escape to Switzerland, and in a plot to try to topple the Nazi government. To save lives, he had to tell some lies. Yet he had enormous loyalty to telling the truth. It was he who wrote the truthful confession of the sins of Germany, including sins of churches that allowed themselves to become supporters of this evil government.[1] The truthful confession led churches, and eventually government leaders, to begin the process of national confession and repentance. The practice of acknowledging error has spread to other governments and become an important practice of peacemaking, healing some of the bitterness from war and massacres.

How could Bonhoeffer be such a strong follower of Jesus and such a believer in telling the truth, and yet justify not telling the Nazis what he knew about Jews hiding and escaping? He wrote an essay about a boy in school being asked by his teacher in front of the whole class whether his father often comes home drunk. The boy knew his father did, but he also sensed that the teacher had no business asking a question so damaging to his father's reputation in front of everyone. So he answered no. Bonhoeffer wrote that the boy understood the meaning of truth in relationship to reality better than the teacher did. He had no covenant with the teacher obligating him to tell about private family matters. Truth is thus a covenant. Bonhoeffer had no covenant relationship with Nazis to tell them where Jews were hiding. Parents have a covenant relation with their children to tell them the truth, but not the part of the truth that is too frightening for them to be able to cope or understand. By contrast, children do have a covenant relation with their parents to tell them the whole truth.

This covenantal understanding is very different from calculating when telling the truth or a lie is to your advantage. Such self-interested calculation opens the door to a life of deceit. In a society where everyone is always calculating whether to tell a lie, trust breaks down and people learn to do only what is in their own selfish interest. People learn to lie to God and deceive themselves. It is a society at war with itself, and at war with God. Telling the truth is a covenant obligation to others in God's presence.

MAKING PEACE

"An eye for an eye and a tooth for a tooth" (Figure 5.2) is taught in Exodus 21:24, Leviticus 24:20, and Deuteronomy 19:21. It limits the amount of retaliation to the same penalty as the damage caused by the attack, instead of what Lamech said at the end of the Cain and Abel story: "If Cain is avenged sevenfold, truly Lamech seventy-sevenfold." Vicious cycles of retaliation happen almost universally in human relations; one example is the suicide bombers of Palestine and the assassination attacks by Israel's military, where both sides believe in punishing each other with escalating violence. But retaliation has increased the violence as well as lasting hatred.

Traditional Righteousness: Retaliation for Injury

Hoping to stop the vicious cycle of retaliation, ancient Israel worked out restorative justice procedures for fines to be paid. Moving farther forward in the direction of peacemaking, Jesus' teaching offered a nonviolent initiative that would deliver people from the cycle of retaliation. Notice, however, that Jesus avoided quoting the "life for a life" part of those three Old Testament teachings. In fact, Jesus never quoted any Old Testament teaching that advocated killing.

The Vicious Cycle: Revenge

The vicious cycle in this teaching is revengeful retaliation. It leads to destruction. The same Clarence Jordan who helped us translate the beatitudes in Chapter Three has pointed out that the Greek word usually translated "evil" in this teaching should actually be translated as "by evil means." Greek grammar makes either meaning equally acceptable. The rule is that we should decide according to which meaning makes most sense in the

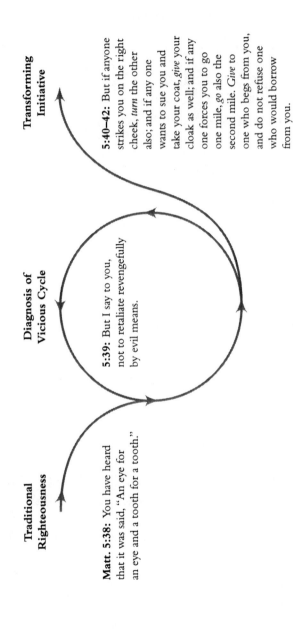

Traditional Righteousness

Matt. 5:38: You have heard that it was said, "An eye for an eye and a tooth for a tooth."

Diagnosis of Vicious Cycle

5:39: But I say to you, not to retaliate revengefully by evil means.

Transforming Initiative

5:40–42: But if anyone strikes you on the right cheek, *turn* the other also; and if any one wants to sue you and take your coat, *give* your cloak as well; and if any one forces you to go one mile, *go* also the second mile. *Give* to one who begs from you, and do not refuse one who would borrow from you.

Figure 5.2. Practices of Peacemaking Initiatives.

context. It makes no sense to think Jesus taught that we should not resist evil; he himself repeatedly resisted the evil of the temple authorities, the scribes and Pharisees, those who were greedy, and Satan. Furthermore, the Greek word usually translated "resist," in "do not resist evil," normally means not to engage in "revengeful or violent retaliation." So the literal translation should be "not to retaliate revengefully by evil means."[2]

The Apostle Paul quotes this same teaching of Jesus in Romans 12:17–21: "Do not repay anyone evil for evil. . . . Beloved, never avenge yourselves. . . . If your enemies are hungry, feed them; if they are thirsty, give them something to drink. . . . Do not overcome evil by evil [means], but overcome evil with good."

The teaching is also echoed in Luke 6:27–36, 1 Thessalonians 5:15, Didache 1:4–5, and 1 Peter 2:21–23. None of them speaks of *not* resisting evil, or refers to an evil person, or mentions renouncing rights in a law court. All emphasize the transforming initiatives of returning good (not evil), using good means (not evil means). First Thessalonians 5:15 says, "See that none of you repays evil for evil, but always seek to do good to one another and to all." This is what Jesus' teaching means. Jesus' focus was on the transforming initiatives we can take to break the cycle of revengeful retaliation.

Transformation and Deliverance: Respond in New and Surprising Ways

The transforming initiatives (Matt. 5:39b–42) show us how to participate in the coming of the reign of God instead of the vicious cycle of revengeful retaliation. This fits Jesus' teaching of the Golden Rule: "Do unto others as you would have others do to you." It commands us to take initiatives such as paying attention to an enemy's valid interests—giving food or drink when the enemy is hungry or thirsty. It breaks up the vicious cycle of violence and counterviolence. Jesus teaches that we should take surprising initiatives, creative and preventive measures that might break up the hatred and distrust, and move toward some degree of justice.

Jesus says that if anyone slaps you on the right cheek, turn the left one too. (In Jesus' culture, it was forbidden to reach out and touch someone with the left hand; the left hand was for dirty things. Soap was not yet available in that time, and people used their left hands for all kinds of dirty tasks. So this would have to be a slap with the right hand.) A slap with the right hand on the right cheek would be a slap with the back of the hand. This would be an insult to someone's honor, the way you would slap a slave, saying "you cur," "you dog," "you have no honor." To turn the other cheek is not simply to put up with the insult; it is to turn the cheek of equal dignity. It may of course lead to a second slap; or it may surprise the arrogant person into realizing you have an unexpected kind of dignity. It is like the followers of Martin Luther King Jr., who did not retaliate against the segregationist racists but marched nonviolently in the face of stones, police dogs, beatings, and fire hoses. This shocked the world into a new kind of awareness of the injustice and a new kind of respect for the self-discipline of the nonviolent protest.

Second, the teachings say, "If anyone wants to sue you for your shirt, let him have your coat, too." The Williams translation and the New English Bible, the New Living Translation, and the Good News Bible (TEV) translate it "shirt and coat," which makes better sense in present-day English than coat and cloak. The point is that you are being sued in court for your *undergarment,* which in plain English is the shirt off your back. You are being sued because you owe some money and cannot pay it. You are so poor that all you have left for possessions are your shirt and your coat. The person suing you cannot sue you for your coat, because that was forbidden in Exodus 22:26–27, Deuteronomy 24:12–13, and Amos 2:8. If you took a man's coat in pledge for a loan, you had to return it every night, else what would he sleep in when it gets cold? So in Jesus' teaching the greedy lender sues you for the only other piece of clothing you have, your shirt. Jesus suggests a shocking transforming initiative: take off your coat and your shirt, and give them both to the greedy person, while standing naked in the law court. In Jesus' culture, that would be enormously embarrassing. It would reveal the plaintiff's greed in all its nakedness.

In the third passage, the context is that in Jesus' time a Roman soldier occupying Judea and Israel had the right to demand that a Jew carry his pack one mile. Jews resented the occupation, and they resented carrying the packs. It was unjust. What to do? The Sicarii, and later the Zealots, advocated violence against the occupying force. It was like Hamas and Islamic Jihad advocating violence against Israel's occupation of Palestine. Jesus advocated a nonviolent initiative: carry the pack a second mile.

In neither case does Jesus say, "Do what he is forcing you to do, comply with oppression, and live with powerless resentment." Instead, he teaches us to do something at our own initiative, under our own power, something that we are not forced to do, something surprising that is in itself a form of resistance. It is a nonviolent initiative that confronts the injustice. It shifts from resentful powerlessness to the power of our own surprising initiative, which also calls our adversary to a new level of consciousness of what he or she is doing. In the segregationist South of the 1950s, blacks felt powerless. Then, in the 1960s, millions carried out boycotts and marches and filled the jails, with amazing self-discipline, with no action of revengeful violence. It turned the segregated world upside down, making a powerful moral appeal to the whole nation's sense of justice.

If we combine Jesus' teaching on the second mile with his teaching on going to the brother to make peace, we can imagine that his disciples, who would carry a Roman soldier's pack two miles, would also engage in conversation on the way, seeking to make peace. Roman soldiers might learn how Jews felt about the occupation, and Jews might learn how Roman soldiers felt about occupying a resentful population. A Jew might ask about the Roman soldier's family, and how it felt to be living far away from home in Italy. We can imagine a Roman centurion asking why the Jew is carrying his pack a second mile. We can imagine the Jew explaining Jesus' way of discipleship and peacemaking, and how Jesus was healing not only hatred against Romans but also the blind, the lepers, and the paralyzed. We can imagine the centurion then going to Jesus and begging him to heal his own child, telling Jesus that he had faith in him, and Jesus commending him for his faith. We can also imagine a centurion later, seeing how Jesus died on the cross, saying, "This must be the Son of God" (see Matt. 8:5–13 and Mark 15:39).

But at the time of Christ, Judah did not make peace; the Jews chose the way of violence and rebellion against Rome that Jesus opposed. It did not work well; Rome responded by making war against Jerusalem, destroying the temple and killing thousands of Jews in 70 A.D., just as Jesus prophesied. As it turned out, the way of loving your enemy and sharing the gospel worked much better. Rome was converted to Christianity by the fourth century.

The fourth transforming initiative turns the tables. Now we, the disciples, are not confronting an oppressor; instead a poor beggar confronts us. Again Jesus calls on us to take a transforming initiative: give to the beggar, and honor a request for a loan. For example, today this might mean giving generously to Wayside Christian Mission, Bread for the World, Save the Children, Catholic Charities, World Vision International, or your four favorite groups that aid the poor and hungry whom you care about. It probably means joining with others to seek justice for the poor, including the working poor, and their children.

Each transforming initiative includes an element of surprise, and some subversive correction of the hostility, domination, exclusion, and injustice that characterize our world. Each is one more mustard seed in the breakthrough of the reign of God in our everyday life. Each brings people distanced and excluded by the desire for revenge, insult, hostility, or injustice into the possibility of covenanting together to work in community. Each is a genuine opportunity in real life to participate in the transformation from separateness to togetherness.

In Jesus' day, Pontius Pilate sneaked Roman banners carrying the image of Caesar (to whom the Romans attributed a kind of divinity) into the city of Jerusalem during the night. This was a huge offense for Jews, because the Ten Commandments forbade making images. In the morning, when people saw the banners, multitudes went to Pilate's palace and petitioned him for six days to take them away. On the sixth day, Pilate had his troops ready, in hiding. Suddenly the troops surrounded the people, with their swords out and ready. Pilate threatened the people with immediate death unless they stopped bothering him with their petitions. The people nonviolently threw themselves on the ground and laid their necks bare. They said they would accept death rather than have the Torah transgressed. Surprised and overwhelmed, Pilate allowed them to live and removed the banners.

The next time they made a similar protest, Pilate had them killed before they could throw themselves on the ground. Later, Caesar Gaius Caligula demanded that people worship him and ordered his statue to be put in the temple at Jerusalem. This time the Jews engaged in a general strike. They left the fields untilled during planting season and gathered to entreat the Roman ruler for more than a month. They committed themselves to nonviolence, and to giving their lives before permitting the sacrilege in the temple. Their action won over the heads of the royal house, and even the Roman ruler in Palestine. The order was withdrawn and the statue was not placed in the temple. This demonstrates clearly that the strategy of nonviolent protest was relevant in Jesus' day.[3]

In our day, a new *just peacemaking ethic* has been developed by scholars representing many denominations, Protestant and Catholic. It incorporates Jesus' way of peacemaking systematically and grows out of realistic awareness that merely debating whether war is right or wrong is not enough. We need an ethic that spells out realistic peacemaking that actually does prevent war and achieves some justice. The just peacemaking ethic identifies ten practices that are rooted in Jesus' teachings and that are in fact working realistically in preventing war in many places.[4] It is gathering widespread support.

One of the ten practices in the just peacemaking ethic is *truthful confession* of our own error and responsibility for injustice and war, as Bonhoeffer did when he led confessions of German error during World War II. Another is *nonviolent direct action,* as was enacted by Jews in Jesus' day. Nonviolent action was effective in the movement for independence in India led by Mahatma Gandhi and Abdul Ghaffar Khan; in the civil rights movement led by Martin Luther King Jr.; in the movement of the people of the Philippines who toppled their dictator, Ferdinand Marcos; in the Solidarity movement in Poland; and in the Revolution of the Candles in East Germany that toppled the Berlin Wall and the dictator Eric Honecker. It has worked in many less-well-known places to remove serious injustice and bring about resolution by nonviolent means.

Another of the practices is *independent initiatives,* which also implements Jesus' teaching of transforming initiatives such as going the second mile. This was the key to the United States and the former Soviet Union getting rid of half of their nuclear weapons and ending the cold war.[5] It is the key to the Roadmap to Peace by which Palestine elected a prime minister other than Yasser Arafat who could work for peace and suspend the suicide bombing, and by which Israel released some prisoners and ended occupation of Gaza and some settlements in the West Bank. Palestine is one of the hardest cases; at the time of this writing nobody knows if they will succeed in taking further independent initiatives in the Roadmap to Peace. But we already see that even in this difficult and long-lasting conflict, it can make a difference. Jesus' way of breakthrough and deliverance can succeed in the real world in which we live.

A fourth practice of just peacemaking that is working to solve conflict in many places is *cooperative conflict resolution.* This implements what Jesus taught: if there is anger between you and someone else, go, talk, and make peace. In the previous chapter, we saw that this often works to make peace and deal with anger within a marriage. It often works as well between nations, solving problems that otherwise might lead to war.

Each of these teachings is meant to show us the way of deliverance as participation in the new things God is doing in our midst. They are about the in-breaking of the reign of God in our lives. Therefore we look for new and creative initiatives that we can pursue in our own context. No Roman soldier is going to demand that we carry his pack a mile, but we may encounter oppressive demands. So we prayerfully create surprising initiatives that hope for the beginning of better relationships. No one is going to demand my shirt in a law court, but someone may try to undermine my reputation. So I pray about deliverance from this vicious cycle. Someone may not slap me on the right cheek but still insult me one way or another. So I develop the habit of replying to an insult by showing dignity and love for the enemy, as Rosa Parks and King did in beginning the civil rights movement. The history of the church shows many examples of Jesus' followers inventing surprising initiatives that defused explosive hostility and began to create more peaceful relationships. (It also shows many examples of "Christians" who failed to follow Jesus, instead adding the fuel of revenge to the vicious cycle of hostility. They usually interpreted this not as transforming initiatives but as idealistic teachings that meant only negative renunciation.)

Some idealistic interpreters have said Jesus aimed at simply teaching absolute ideals. But we know that Jesus strove for results, in the form of repentance and deliverance. He regularly called on people to repent, because God's reign is beginning to happen and we can participate joyfully. We know that he sought to create community between us and others we are separated from. Similarly, in the twelfth chapter of Romans the Apostle Paul says that by giving some food and drink to our enemy we can "heap coals of fire on his head." This does not mean we can burn a hole in his brain; it means we can get him to repent. It was an ancient custom, when repenting, to put on sackcloth and carry a bowl of ashes on one's head with hot coals, so it would give off the smoke of repentance. These initiatives seek repentance, forgiveness, and new community where there is hostility and separateness.

Jesus' teachings are realistically purpose-driven: go, be reconciled to your brother; and make friends quickly with your accuser, lest your accuser hand you over to the judge and you be put in prison (Matt. 5:25). "Love your enemies and pray for your persecutors," so that you may be children of your Father who makes his sun rise on the evil and the good (Matt. 5:44–45). "Your Father who sees in secret will reward you" (6:1–18). If you forgive people their trespasses, God will forgive you (6:14). Do not give dogs what is holy, lest they trample it under foot and turn to attack you (7:6). "Ask, and it will be given you" (7:7). "Not everyone who says to me 'Lord, Lord' will enter the kingdom of heaven, but only the one who does the will of my Father in heaven" (7:21).

It is true that Jesus' teachings are grace-driven. They are also based on the presence of God's mercy, God's love, God's bringing God's reign into our daily lives. They are purpose-driven, practical deliverance as well.

LOVING OUR ENEMIES

In Matthew 5:43–48, the sentence, "You shall love your neighbor and hate your enemy," does not come from the Old Testament. It comes from the scrolls of the Qumran Community, which lived down by the Dead Sea in Jesus' time. See Figure 5.3.

The Vicious Cycle: Easy Love

Loving only those who love you is the in-group selfishness of cliquishness, cronyism, nepotism, racism, and nationalism. We

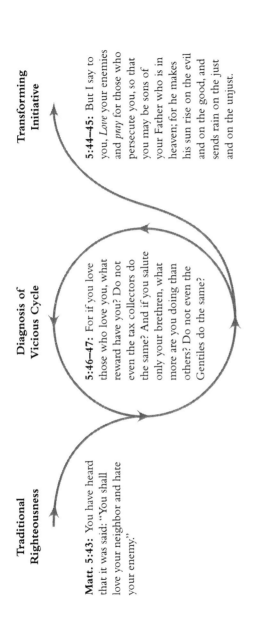

Traditional Righteousness

Matt. 5:43: You have heard that it was said: "You shall love your neighbor and hate your enemy."

Diagnosis of Vicious Cycle

5:46–47: For if you love those who love you, what reward have you? Do not even the tax collectors do the same? And if you salute only your brethren, what more are you doing than others? Do not even the Gentiles do the same?

Transforming Initiative

5:44–45: But I say to you, *Love* your enemies and *pray* for those who persecute you, so that you may be sons of your Father who is in heaven; for he makes his sun rise on the evil and on the good, and sends rain on the just and on the unjust.

Figure 5.3. Loving Your Enemy.

recognize it immediately because we see it so often. If we love only those who love us, we see only an in-group perspective, and become closed-minded to how others see things. As a result, we cannot understand our enemies' perspectives enough to deal with them effectively. We are less effective, less powerful, because we do not sufficiently understand enemies who wish us harm and so cannot do what is effective in persuading them to do what we think is right. We grow frustrated and blame them all the more. We transfer our ineffectiveness to other people whom we do not understand. This is the powerlessness of a culture of blame.

In Jesus' day, the Pharisees advocated purity by meal rituals that excluded anyone who had not washed himself in a pre-scribed way (symbolizing riddance of outside contacts). Tax collectors, women, Gentiles, impure people, and those who did not practice ritual washing were all excluded. They also taught that strictly practicing "tithing"—giving to charity a tenth of every-thing you have to eat—was essential for purity and righteous-ness. No one could join the meal who was not tithing even the dill, mint, and cumin used for seasoning. Jesus was deeply wor-ried that the Pharisees' practice of excluding outsiders and blaming corruption on foreigners led to hate against Romans and violent rebellion against Roman soldiers. Jesus said, "Woe to you, scribes and Pharisees, hypocrites! For you tithe mint, dill, and cumin, and you have neglected the weightier matters of the law: justice and mercy and faithfulness. . . . You blind guides! You strain out a gnat but swallow a camel!" (Matt. 23:23).

The Pharisees and the scribes taught that holiness means separateness and exclusion. Jesus taught that holiness means com-passion and mercy. He purposely ate with tax collectors, women, even prostitutes, in an intentional reversal of the Pharisaic prac-tice. He called on all of us—ourselves, Jews, and even the Pharisees—to repent because what defiles us more than pollu-tion coming into us from outside is the envy, slander, deceit, greed, and killing that come from the heart in its hateful rela-tions with others (Mark 7:18–22).

This is a clue to the meaning of Jesus' saying that our righteousness should exceed that of the Pharisees; it should surpass them in including others in our community of neighbor love.

Transformation and Deliverance:
Love Your Neighbor as Yourself

"You shall love your neighbor as yourself" comes from Leviticus 19:17–18. But the question people discussed in Jesus' time was, "Who is included in our community of neighbors?" (Luke 10:29).

Jesus answers by pointing out that God gives sunshine and rain even to God's enemies. Therefore we are to participate in what God is doing, to be children of our Father in heaven. We are to include even our enemies in the community of neighbors to whom we give love.

Love, biblically, is more than an attitude or a feeling. It includes action seeking to meet the valid needs of the other. Here Jesus calls on us to pray for our enemies and greet (or salute) them. In Paul's presentation of this teaching in Romans 12, he calls on us to feed our enemies when they are hungry and give them something to drink when they are thirsty; to grieve with them when they grieve and rejoice with them when they rejoice. This does not mean we affirm everything our enemies do; Jesus often confronted Pharisees and other leaders and their injustices. It means our enemies have some valid needs to which we can say yes.

"Love your enemies," of Jesus' teachings the one most often quoted in early Christian writings, is recognized by most New Testament scholars as Jesus' initiative and central in his teaching. It is also especially relevant to the time in which he lived, when most Jews would have thought of their Roman occupiers as enemies, not neighbors.

In Jesus' time, anger was building against Rome's occupation of the Jewish homeland and heavy taxation. Now and then, a false Messiah would gather some followers to rebel and would then be assassinated by the Romans. We experience something like this when we see Palestinians resenting Israel for occupying their homeland. Jesus warned against such hatred toward enemies and wept over Jerusalem because its leaders did not know the practices that make for peace. He warned repeatedly that the temple would be destroyed, and taught that when the war came his followers should flee into the hills rather than take part. He called for actions of love and peacemaking toward Romans and tax collectors. Jesus treated Roman centurions with respect, and even praise for their faith, and he welcomed tax collectors such as Matthew into the community of the disciples.

Our time also sees the threat of war and destruction. Now we have the enormous peril of nuclear, chemical, and biological weapons and terrorism. Does Jesus' action of including enemies in the community of discussion and mutual concern point to a way of deliverance amid these real threats?

The new just peacemaking ethic has noticed that nations that participate extensively in international networks with other nations—through travel, trade, mail and e-mail, through exchange students and missionaries, respect for treaties, and visits and memberships in international groups of all kinds— make war less often. Building a network of relationships that include even enemies in the community of discussion and exchange tends to reduce the drive toward war, and increase understanding and shared loyalty. Similarly, those countries cooperating extensively with the UN and its various agencies tend to make war less often. Regularly discussing concerns and issues with representatives of other nations, and regularly being connected in various kinds of community with them, decreases the frequency of making war. This makes sense in terms of Jesus' teaching that we are to build community even with enemies.

Two practices of just peacemaking are therefore to "work with cooperative forces in the international system" and "strengthen the United Nations and international efforts for cooperation and human rights."[6]

Jesus' teachings once again are the way of deliverance in the real world of hatred and war. Let us look at just one example where these two practices of just peacemaking made the difference. In the late 1990s, the demagogic leader of Serbia, Milosevic, made war—against Bosnia, then Croatia, and finally Kosovo. The Serbian uprising in Bosnia massacred large numbers of Muslims. The war against Catholic Croatia replayed historic atrocities. The outcome was enormous bitterness and hostility among the ethnic and religious factions there—Serbian Orthodox, Croatian Catholic, and Bosnian Muslim—and fear that they could hardly live together in the future. But the international forces of the North Atlantic Treaty Organization were crucial in achieving the truce and policing it so that new uprisings would not occur. Relations now are far from perfect, but they are much better thanks to cooperative forces in the international system.

Then Serbia attacked Kosovo and, in a campaign of ethnic cleansing, drove most of the Albanian-Muslim-Kosovars from their homes. The United States and other NATO countries threatened the Serbian forces with bombing if they did not cease their ethnic cleansing and leave. But they refused. So the bombing started in the spring of 1999. U.S. policymakers thought the Serbs would quickly see their cause was hopeless and leave; they had no defense against the enormously superior U.S. and NATO forces. But they still refused to leave. As the bombing began, I wrote an article in *Sojourners* magazine applying just peacemaking ethics. Conflict resolution said that to get Serbia out we needed to pay attention to Serbian concerns, which was the defense of Serbian civilians who lived in Kosovo and the Serbian churches and historical places there. Serbia saw NATO as their enemy and did not want to evacuate Kosovo and leave it in the grip of NATO forces. A solution was for the occupying forces to include Russians, who were friendlier to Serbia; and the occupation would need to be under UN authorization, not NATO's.

The U.S. forces were surprised when the bombing lasted for months and the Serbs still did not retreat. Finally, NATO got a

new president (from Finland), who announced that the occupying forces would include Russian troops, and he put the
occupation under UN authorization. The very next day, the
Serbs began withdrawing. I wrote the article near the beginning of the bombing, so it was a test of the realism of just
peacemaking practice of working with international forces and
the United Nations. Just peacemaking proved right. International cooperation in the just peacemaking ethic stopped the
war and allowed the people of Kosovo to return to their
homes. Resentment and the danger of violence are still there;
but people are once again living in their own homes, and violence is restrained.

CONCLUSION: BE COMPLETE AND INCLUSIVE IN YOUR LOVE

Jesus' teaching of love for enemies, including them in the community of neighbors whom we are to love, is the climax of the
first six teachings in Matthew 5:21–48. Other climaxes come in
Matthew 5:16, 6:14–16, 7:12, and 7:28–29. In each case, the end
of a section is signaled in three ways:

1. The pattern of teaching is a bit different. In this case, the
   vicious cycle (Matt. 5:46–47) comes *after* the transforming
   initiative (5:44–45) rather than before it.
2. A summarizing explanation is given: "Be complete, therefore, as your heavenly Father is complete" (Matt. 5:48).
3. Jesus points to God's presence, mercy, and love. It is striking how central God's mercy and presence are in the
   Sermon on the Mount. We shall see this again and again.

I translate Matthew 5:48 as "Be complete, therefore, as your heavenly Father is complete," not "Be perfect, therefore, as your heavenly Father is perfect" (the more common translation), for

three reasons. First, this teaching is about God's completeness in including the evil and the good, the unrighteous and the righteousness, in God's love. God is complete and all-inclusive, giving sunshine and rain to all, even enemies. The teaching is not about God being perfect in the sense of living up to some ideal of perfection, as the English word *perfect* suggests. It is about the completeness of God's love.

Second, Luke 6:36 gives us the same teaching. There Jesus says, "Be merciful, as your Father is merciful." The point is not that God lives up to some ideal of perfection, but that God is merciful, "kind to the ungrateful and the wicked" (Luke 6:35).

Finally, the Greek *teleios* can mean perfect, or it can mean whole, undivided, complete. It is a translation of the Hebrew *tamim*. Neither the Greek word nor the Hebrew is ever applied to God in the Old Testament or in the Dead Sea Scrolls. Thus if the word is taken to mean living up to high ideals of perfection, it would not make sense to say so of God. There are no high ideals of perfection by which God is measured; God is higher than all our ideals ("As the heavens are higher than the earth, so are my ways higher than your ways and my thoughts than your thoughts"; Isa. 55:8–9). It makes perfect sense to say that God is complete in love, including even enemies in the community of God's mercy. In fact, this is exactly what Matthew 5:45 and 48 say. This fits perfectly with Jesus' and Isaiah's teaching that holiness is seen in redemptive compassion rather than in being separate from whatever is unclean (Matt. 12:11–12; Luke 13:1–16, 14:5).

Far from a teaching that we are to live up to high Greek ideals of perfection, it is that we are to be complete in our love, including all persons in our community of neighbors whom we love. We are to be merciful as God is merciful.

6

The Prayer of Jesus

The Jesus Prayer, which is usually referred to as the Lord's
Prayer, is certainly well and widely known for its beauty
and profundity. But our very familiarity creates a problem: we may not let it stimulate our imagination in new direc-
tions as we pray. Jesus warns us, "Do not heap up empty phrases"
as we pray (Matt. 6:7). How can we fill this prayer with the true
content that Jesus intended, content that connects with our own
real concerns and experiences? How can we pray Jesus' Prayer
in a new way?

The first step is to base our praying in Jesus' own life and his
respect for the prophets of Israel. That is my goal in this chapter. It is also why I prefer to call it Jesus' Prayer rather than the
traditional Lord's Prayer. The second step is to notice that Jesus
does not simply say, "Pray exactly these words, again and again."
He says pray "in this way"—similarly, not identically. You can
practice praying to God in your own words, no matter how
simple they are. As opposed to fancy words, or many words, or
lots of repetition without much content, this is praying with
your own real feelings and imagination.

Matthew 6:1–18 begins with a teaching on giving to the
poor and ends with one on fasting. They enfold Jesus' two
teachings on prayer like a pair of praying hands. All four teachings share a similar pattern of transformation and deliverance
that we have come to know (Figure 6.1).

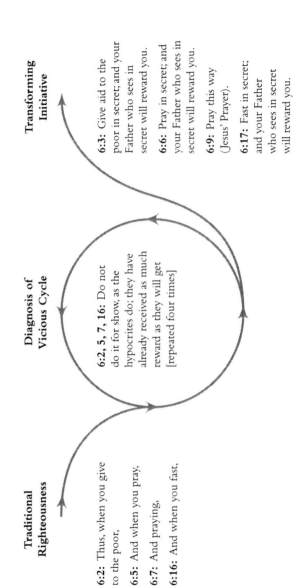

Traditional Righteousness

6:2: Thus, when you give to the poor,

6:5: And when you pray,

6:7: And praying,

6:16: And when you fast,

Diagnosis of Vicious Cycle

6:2, 5, 7, 16: Do not do it for show, as the hypocrites do; they have already received as much reward as they will get [repeated four times]

Transforming Initiative

6:3: Give aid to the poor in secret; and your Father who sees in secret will reward you.

6:6: Pray in secret; and your Father who sees in secret will reward you.

6:9: Pray this way (Jesus' Prayer).

6:17: Fast in secret; and your Father who sees in secret will reward you.

Figure 6.1. Practices of Righteousness.

PRACTICES OF RIGHTEOUSNESS

Giving to the poor, praying, and fasting were the three traditional practices of righteousness in Judaism. Although some of our bibles translate the first verse as "Beware of practicing your *piety,*" this word is translated "righteousness" in "hunger and thirst for righteousness" and throughout the Sermon on the Mount (Matt. 5:5, 10, 20, and 6:33).

Traditional Righteousness: Seeking Restorative Justice

In Chapter Three on the beatitudes, we saw that the word does not mean the self-righteousness that an individual can possess. It actually means "restorative justice" or "delivering justice" (rescuing the powerless and outcasts, restoring them to their rightful place in covenant community).

Giving to the poor is a practice of this kind of delivering, restorative justice. Similarly, *praying to God,* who cares deeply for justice for the powerless, attunes us to God's will for deliverance. *Fasting* helps us identify with the hungry of the earth and repent for our greed and lack of concern. These three practices of righteousness or restorative justice participate in God's compassion for the needy or people who are being treated unjustly.

The Vicious Cycle: Righteousness for the Wrong Reason

In each case, Jesus warns against succumbing to the temptation, the vicious cycle, of practicing righteousness for show and expecting a reward from God. We remember Jesus' parable in which the self-righteous Pharisee was praying, fasting, and giving alms (tithing) for show, apparently praying out loud about how much better he was than others. By contrast, the tax collector "beat his breast, saying, 'God, be merciful to me a sinner!' (Luke 18:10–14). We notice that Jesus' Prayer is a lot more like the humble prayer of the tax collector than the self-righteous prayer of the Pharisee. It asks for forgiveness and resistance to temptation.

Transformation and Deliverance: Righteousness for God Alone

In each teaching, Jesus gives us a transforming initiative—to practice in secret, in God's knowing and merciful presence.

If Jesus had taught that we should pray noisily on street corners and in church, while thinking only of God and never about what others make of our conduct, then this would have been a hard teaching to live. In the presence of others, we naturally consider what others think. The same is true about giving to charity and fasting: if Jesus had taught that we should make a lot of noise about how much we give or how often we fast, mindful only of God's presence and never what others think, that would have been impossible. We do worry about what others think of us. If we are prideful people like the Pharisee, we think about it a lot.

Jesus taught a highly practical way to be delivered from the problem of trying to impress others. When we pray, we are to do so secretly, in our own room with the door shut. Then it is easier to think about God's will and presence, without worrying about what others think of our words. We can also confess more truthfully and ask God's real guidance more openly, even tearfully.

In all four teachings, Jesus concludes by pointing to God's presence, compassionate mercy, and deliverance, just as the prophet Isaiah does. The characteristics of the reign of God that we saw—God's presence, compassion, and deliverance—are central throughout the Sermon. Jesus really is fulfilling the promise of the coming of God's reign that we saw in Chapters One and Two.

JESUS' PRAYER:
THE ORGANIZING CENTER
OF THE SERMON ON THE MOUNT

Matthew 5:1–48	*Jesus' Prayer*	*Matthew 6:19–7:27*
5:1–2 Jesus teaches on the mountain, like Moses on Mount Sinai	Our Father in heaven, hallowed be Your Name	
5:3–16 Beatitudes: joy because we participate in the reign that is coming	Your reign come	
5:17–48 The better righteousness of the first six triads	Your will be done on earth as in heaven	
	Give us today our daily bread	**6:19–34** Do not anxiously hoard treasures, food, and clothes
	Forgive us our sins	**7:1–5** Judge not; take the log out of your own eye
	Lead us not into temptation	**7:6–12** Do not put your trust in the dogs and pigs, but in God
	But deliver us from evil	**7:13–27** Beware of false prophets

Jesus' Prayer comes at the center of the Sermon on the Mount, between the teachings of Matthew 5:1–48 and the teachings of Matthew 6:19–7:27. It occupies the commanding position, the pivotal spot.

Many biblical passages locate their high point in the center, the heart of the passage. The central pivot often contains references to all the main points that come before and after it, serving as the organizing center of the whole passage.

So the question arises: Are the seven petitions of Jesus' Prayer, coming in the middle of the Sermon on the Mount, the organizing center of the whole sermon? I think the answer is yes, and in a striking way. Noticing how Jesus' Prayer is related to the whole sermon helps us understand each of the seven petitions of the prayer more richly and concretely. In what follows, I will show how each petition relates to a section of the Sermon on the Mount, step by step.

Our Father in Heaven

Jesus' Prayer begins, "Our Father." Speaking to God as "our Father" points to Jesus' closeness to God, and to God's presence in our lives, delivering us from disobedience to obedience and from distance to presence. Through Jesus, we too can have that closeness; Jesus clearly teaches us to pray to our Father. Our Father who sees in secret knows what we need before we ask him (Matt. 6:4 and 6:6). This is a fulfillment of Isaiah's promise of God's presence.

When Jesus teaches us to pray to "our Father," he is pointing to God's compassion as well as God's presence. When he speaks of God's holy "name," he is pointing to the name of God revealed in Exodus 3, 6, and 20—Yahweh who hears our cries and delivers us, redeems us.

My wife and I were once the resident advisors for twenty-seven bright women students at a university dormitory. They asked me to be part of their process of asking probing questions on the meaning of life and the ethics they wanted to follow for the rest of their lives. It was a wonderful and memorable experience for all of us. They were intellectually as well as spiritually engaged, and their grades soared. Their experiment continued in the following years, spreading to creation of other focus dorms.

Halfway through the year, as I was getting to know them deeper and deeper, it finally dawned on me: very few of them had a truly functioning father in their family. Either their parents were divorced or their father was a workaholic or alcoholic and not really present. To extrapolate, this pervasive absence of "good fathers" in our society has led some people to pray to "Our Mother who art in heaven," or "Our Parent who art in heaven," or even "Our Grandparent who art in heaven." Many others identify with Jesus' picture of what our Father in heaven is like, and the identification helps heal the pain from the missing father on earth in their lives. In all these cases, God's compassionate presence is the key; it is the meaning. I believe this is right and true to God's character, and to God's will as revealed in Jesus.

In all four teachings in Matthew 6:1–18, Jesus refers to "your Father *in heaven*"; Jesus' Prayer begins, "Our Father *in heaven*." This does not mean distant and separated from us. Heaven, biblically, means the realm where God rules fully and God's will is done. Jesus is affirming that God really is the Ruler, and that God really is our Father, present, bringing deliverance into our lives. In the conclusion of all four triads, and throughout the Sermon on the Mount, Jesus makes it clear that our Father shows mercy and deliverance here on earth, in our very lives.

The prophet Isaiah may give us a clue for Jesus' prayer to "our Father in heaven, hallowed be your name." Four passages in Isaiah (9:2–7, 45:9–17, 63:15–19, 64:7–9) refer to God as *Father*; they also speak of God *in heaven,* and of God's *name.* In Isaiah 45, God asserts God's name eight times as "I am the Lord" (Yahweh) or "I the Lord," and seven other times as "the Lord."

Here is Isaiah 63:15–19: "Look down from *heaven* and see, from your holy and glorious habitation. Where are your zeal and your might? The yearning of your heart and your compassion? They are withheld from me. For you are *our father* . . . ; you, O

Lord, are *our father, our Redeemer from of old is your name.* Why,
O Lord, do you make us stray from your ways, and harden our
heart, so that we do not fear you? . . . We have long been like
those whom you do not rule, like those not called by *your name.*"

All four Isaiah passages speak of the people being disobedi-
ent to God and of God's distance from us (for example, having
hidden his face from us in darkness). They all speak of God's
coming to us and being present to redeem us. God's hallowed
name is seen in "I AM the LORD," the Redeemer who delivers us. Jesus' Prayer calls on God to deliver us from our disobedience and our sense of God's distance, and to be present to us
as the Father who loves us. This is why again and again in the
Sermon on the Mount Jesus speaks of God being present with
mercy and love, knowing what we need even before we ask, and
giving us good gifts.

In his wonderful book *Praying Like Jesus,* James Mulholland
writes that the prayer of Jesus is hugely different from the recently popularized prayer of Jabez, which is all about me, me, me:
"Bless me and enlarge my territory. Let your hand be with me,
and keep me from harm so I will be free from pain." This makes
my prayer into a magic device for getting what I want. Mulholland says, "The proper attitude is a matter of humility and trust.
Do we recognize our utter dependence upon God? Do we trust
God to faithfully meet our needs?"[1]

Hallowed Be Your Name

Jesus' Prayer is thoroughly Jewish; so is the meaning of "hallowed be your name." In synagogue worship, during Jesus' time
or soon after, the congregation regularly prayed the Kaddish
prayer, with words like those Jesus prayed, especially emphasizing the name of God:

> Exalted and hallowed be his great name
> in the world which he created according to his will.
> May he let his kingdom rule
> in your lifetime and in your days

and in the lifetime of the whole house of Israel,
speedily and soon.
Praised be his great name from eternity to eternity.
And to this say: Amen.

Both in the Kaddish prayer and in Jesus' Prayer, we pray that
God will let God's name be hallowed. It is God's action of deliverance, making God's reign come; and it is also our active participation, honoring God's name. When God's name is hallowed,
people treat God's name as holy.

In the Kaddish, we pray that God's reign will happen in the
lifetime of fellow synagogue members and "the whole house of
Israel." So it is for the whole people, not only individual benefit. Jesus' Prayer is like that: we pray for *our* daily bread, *our* forgiveness, *our* deliverance. It corrects the individualistic focus of
much popular culture and affirms our shared common good.

Calling on God by name tells us who God is. Mulholland
tells this story:

> When my brother was five years old, he got separated from
> my mother in a grocery store. . . . He was alone in an aisle
> with shelves towering above him and strangers all around
> him. My mother didn't realize he was lost until she heard his
> quivering voice calling out, "Helen, Helen!"
>
> My mother quickly found him, hugged him, and wiped
> away his tears. Then she asked, "Why did you call me Helen?"
>
> My brother replied, "I knew there were lots of mommies
> here, but I thought there would only be one Helen."[2]

Knowing the name is important. Praying "Hallowed be your
name" recalls God's holy name being revealed to Moses on the
mountain at the burning bush, and also when God gave the Ten
Commandments (Exod. 3, 6, 19, and 20). Making the connection
can tell us a lot about the meaning of "Hallowed be your name."

At the burning bush on Mt. Sinai, God revealed God's hallowed name as Yahweh, the LORD, the I AM, who delivers you.
The Israelites were groaning under their slavery in Egypt; they

needed deliverance. Moses asked God what he should tell the Israelites if they ask him, "What is his name?" God answered: "I AM WHO I AM. . . . Thus you shall say to the Israelites, 'I AM has sent me to you'. . . . The LORD (Yahweh), the God of your ancestors, the God of Abraham, the God of Isaac, and the God of Jacob has sent me to you: This is my name forever, and this is my title for all generations" (Exod. 3:13–16). When Abraham, Isaac, and Jacob found themselves in dire straits, God was their Deliverer.

God tells Moses five times that he will be faithful to his covenant with Abraham, Isaac, and Jacob (Exod. 2:25; 3:6, 15; 6:3, 8). Five times God tells Moses, "I will be with you," or "I will deliver you from the oppression of the Egyptians" (3:8, 10, 12, 17; 6:6–8). So God's name means "I will be present with you, I will deliver you, and I will be faithful to my covenant with you."

Five times as well we are told that God experiences the suffering of the oppressed with compassion: "Their cry for help rose up to God and God heard their groaning . . . , and God took notice of them. . . . 'I have observed the misery of my people who are in Egypt; I have heard their cry on account of their taskmasters. Indeed, I know their sufferings'" (Exod. 2:23–25; 3:7, 9, 16; 6:5). So God's name also means God is present to hear the cries of the oppressed and see their misery. This is why throughout the Psalms and the prophets we pray that God will hear our cries, see our suffering, and be present to deliver us.

Yet another theme: Moses removes his shoes, for this is holy ground; and Moses is afraid and hides his face (Exod. 3:5–6). The LORD is mighty and majestic; holy both in the sense of having compassion for the oppressed and delivering them, and also in the sense of having the might to deliver them: "O LORD, our Sovereign, how majestic is your name in all the earth!" (Psalm 8:9).

After God fulfilled his promise and delivered the people of Israel from their slavery in Egypt, "Moses went up to God" on the mountain once again (Exod. 19:3), where he received the Ten Commandments: "There was thunder and lightning, as well as a thick cloud on the mountain. . . . Now Mount Sinai was wrapped in smoke, because the Lord had descended upon it in fire; the smoke went up like the smoke of a kiln, while the whole mountain shook violently. . . ."

We can hardly miss the majesty of God and the hallowedness of the mountain. This is the revelation of the hallowed name of God. There on the holy mountain, God spoke these words:

> I am
> the Lord your God,
> Who brought you out of the land of Egypt,
> out of the house of slavery [Exod. 20:1–2].

Each line gives a parallel meaning in differing words. "I am" is God's name that was revealed at the burning bush, as also is "The LORD." The LORD is the "I AM" in the sense of being present to deliver. This is the LORD's character, the One who delivers the oppressed out of Egypt, out of slavery.

Now we see that "hallowed be your name" in the beginning of Jesus' Prayer connects with Moses going up on the mountain, where God's holy name was revealed. It also connects with Jesus going up onto the mountain as a new Moses at the beginning of the Sermon on the Mount. When you pray, "hallowed be your name," think of the character of God as revealed to Moses and in Jesus. Picture God revealing God's name to Moses as the Deliverer from oppression and the bringer of deliverance. Picture God being present in the teaching, the compassion, the mercy, the justice for the poor and powerless, and the healings, of Jesus.

Your Kingdom Come

Many people are vague when they pray "your kingdom come" or "your reign come" because they lack a clear idea of the characteristics of God's kingdom. But now we see that this petition connects with the seven characteristics of God's reign (Chapter

Two), and with Jesus' teaching of the beatitudes (Chapter Three). We have seen that God's reign brings deliverance and salvation, presence, restorative justice, peace, healing, joy, repentance, and return to God. Now we can fill this petition of Jesus' Prayer with more content. We pray for God's reign to come with those seven characteristics, and with the joy and the meaning of the beatitudes.

We have seen how the beatitudes are about the joy of participation in the reign of God. We experience joy because God acts to deliver us, and because we can be part of what the Creator of the universe is doing in bringing redemption and deliverance. The beatitudes celebrate participation in the coming reign: we will be comforted by God, inherit the earth, be filled with delivering justice, receive God's compassion, see God, be called children of God, and have great reward in God. All these are rewards of participating in God's reign. This experience is already beginning in Jesus. Jesus says we are blessed because God is not distant and absent; we experience God's reign and presence in our midst, and will experience it even more in the future.

So the prayer "your kingdom come" has special meaning because it points to Jesus' teaching about the reign of God in the beatitudes. When you pray "your kingdom come," think of the joy of participation in the joys and the surrender to God's ways of the beatitudes.

But followers of Jesus who pray for God's reign become all the more aware that what is happening in our society is far from God's reign. Their prayer life compares God's compassion for all people with the suffering, violence, injustice, lack of caring, and they become realistic about the cause of what is going wrong. They want to end their sinning and serve God. They want to share in a community that begins to experience the mustard seeds of the kingdom, the small daily breakthroughs of God's reign.

When you pray "your kingdom come," pray for repentance for the persecution and lack of justice, peace, compassion, and integrity. Pray for surrender to God's will, for dedication to working for God's mercy, justice, peacemaking, and integrity.

The German theologian Helmut Thielicke, who lived through the bombing and destruction of World War II, preached in the choir of the church in Stuttgart because the church itself had been reduced to rubble in the air raids. Repeatedly he asked, "How can God allow this to happen?"

He warned that "we must not think of this mysterious growth of God's kingdom (it really is a mystery!) as a kind of evolutionary development. We must not think of it as a gradual Christianization of the world which will increasingly eliminate evil." All around us is evidence of the destruction of faith in human nature. We cannot simply congratulate ourselves on the goodness of human being. He went on:

> May I tell you how I myself have come to feel and experience the reality of God's rule in these days of catastrophe, to feel it in all its mysterious hiddenness, and also in that hiddenness which is so oppressive that it almost reduces one to despair? . . .
>
> I have known moments—like everybody else—in which discouragement crept into my heart and I felt utterly stricken. My work in Stuttgart seemed to have gone to pieces; and my listeners were scattered to the four winds; the churches lay in rubble and ashes. On one occasion when I was absorbed in these gloomy thoughts I was looking down into the concrete pit of a cellar which had been shattered by a bomb and in which more than fifty young persons had been killed. A woman came up to me and . . . said, "My husband died down there. His place was right under the hole. The clean-up squad was unable to find a trace of him; all that was left was his cap. We were there the last time you preached in the cathedral church. And here before this pit I want to thank you for preparing him for eternity."

All of a sudden God had opened a door to his kingdom in the moment of catastrophe and in the midst of the collapse of the personal worlds of two persons. There it was between that woman and myself. I could not express this at the time, of course, because the words simply did not come to me.[3]

To pray that "your kingdom come" is also to pray for repentance and for truly following Jesus. It is to pray for a life that gives thanks for the mustard seeds of the kingdom that happen in the midst of wrong, and a life that participates in Jesus' way.

Your Will Be Done on Earth as in Heaven

The third petition prays, "Your will be done on earth as it is in heaven." Jesus teaches God's will in the main section after the beatitudes, with its six transforming initiatives (Matt. 5:17–48)—a righteousness that is more loving and peacemaking than the righteous exclusiveness of the Pharisees.

When you pray that the will of God be done on earth as it is in heaven, envision conflict being resolved, marriages and families healed, truth told and people faithful to one another, initiatives that break through the vicious cycles of retaliation, and love that creates new community among people through forgiveness, reconciliation, and peacemaking. The will of God, as it is announced in the teachings of the Sermon on the Mount, directs us toward breakthroughs of this kind. Envision yourself participating in such breakthroughs personally.

We have learned about the meaning of God's name by paying attention to the revelation of it in the book of Exodus. We learned about the meaning of the reign of God by paying attention to the prophet whom Jesus quoted again and again, Isaiah. Jesus' six teachings about the will and merciful righteousness of God in Matthew 5:17–48 were his explanation of how to obey the Ten Commandments: do not murder, do not commit adultery, do not use the name of the Lord in vain by bearing false witness, and love your enemy as you love your neighbor. We see that the meaning of Jesus' prayer is consistently filled with content as we root it in the Old Testament as interpreted by Jesus. It is indeed like the Jewish Kaddish prayer.

All three petitions—that God's name be hallowed, God's reign come, and God's will be done—are petitions: "Please, God, bring your deliverance to the earth. As we pray these petitions, we are aware that things are wrong on earth now." We pray, "Please bring about a breakthrough of your reign and your will. The will of God is the will of the Father of Jesus Christ for all the earth, for humankind. Let it be done on earth as it is in heaven."

Give Us Today Our Daily Bread

The first three petitions of Jesus' Prayer are the "you" petitions. They focus on God and delivering action. They ask, "Please bring *your* reign, *your* deliverance." The next four petitions are the "we" petitions. They ask, "Please bring your deliverance *to us.*" Again, they are not just about "me." They are about deliverance coming to us, the community, to us together.

Notice that they are all about God bringing *deliverance,* once again reinforcing that the Sermon on the Mount, through and through, is not prohibitions; it is about God's deliverance. The first petition in the prayer is about deliverance from hunger and basic need.

The word that is usually translated *daily* bread does not appear in any literature of that time, and scholars are not sure what it means. Probably its meaning comes from God's giving the people who were fleeing from Egypt in the wilderness their *daily* Manna or bread (Exod. 16). Moses told them they should gather only as much as they could eat in one day; the next day God would provide more. They did not trust in God and hoarded more than a day's worth; it bred worms and became foul.

The Book of Revelation also promises to fulfill basic needs for those who trust in God and follow Jesus—acting in love, faith, service, and patient endurance. To them "I will give some of the hidden manna" (Rev. 2:2, 17, 19). A prayer for daily bread is thus a prayer for the basic needs of the day, and a prayer for faithfulness and trust in God.

This is what Jesus teaches in Matthew 6:19–34. In a simple paraphrase: Do not hoard for yourself on earth, but put your investments in heaven (in God's will). Do not worry about what you will eat or what you will wear. Doesn't your Father in heaven provide for the birds of the air and the flowers in the field? God knows you need basic things such as food and clothes, and will provide for you. Put your efforts into God's reign and God's restorative justice and people will have all they need and more.

Seeing the meaning of Jesus' teaching in the passage about not hoarding (Matt. 6:19–34) enables us to fill in this petition of Jesus' Prayer more fully. It means that when we pray for our daily bread, we pray for our own basic needs, for our own commitment to justice and fairness and God's reign, and for the community to take care of people who have basic needs.

And Forgive Us Our Debts, as We Also Have Forgiven Our Debtors

We can be brief because the meaning of each of these "we" petitions is to be filled out more fully in the following chapters, as we interpret the meaning of the next sections of the Lord's Prayer that correspond to each petition. Forgiveness, which is essential for the life of the follower of Jesus, deserves space of its own as Chapter Eight. Forgiveness is not simple. It entails four steps:

1. It faces the reality that a wrong or injustice, something hurtful or harmful, did happen. It does not pretend that nothing wrong happened. If nothing wrong happened, there would be no need for forgiveness.

2. It is the way of deliverance that helps overcome the vicious cycle of bitterness and seeking revenge in which many people get stuck.

3. It is usually based on some kind of sharing of feelings or empathy—the awareness that I too have caused a hurt against

someone else sometime in the past, or that I can develop understanding for the guilty person, even if not for the hurtful deed.

4. If forgiveness is complete, it states willingness to restore relationships, to have some kind of community with the guilty person. Of course, this is not possible where the guilty person still threatens violence against the one who is hurt. Then at least, there is a sense of community that comes from knowing that we share a common need, or that the other person was also hurt in the past.

Jesus teaches us to pray, "forgive us *our* debts as we have forgiven our debtors." We recognize that we are sinners ourselves, and therefore we share at least that much with the guilty person.[4]

And Lead Us Not into Temptation, but Deliver Us from Evil

Some scholars (and at least one Bible translation, the NRSV) prefer to render this as "Lead us not into testing" because, they point out, God does not lead us into temptation. But most of us know that we are somehow led into temptation, even if not by God. There are evil forces in life; Jesus is clear about that.[5] For us it is a question of our needing God's deliverance from the temptations and tests that definitely come our way.

We know one thing more: if we spend all our effort on our own white-knuckled struggle against a temptation, it grows bigger and bigger. If instead we shift our attention to the guidance that God gives us, then we are likely to do better. This insight fits Jesus' emphasis on the transforming initiatives of God's grace that rescue us or deliver us from vicious cycles.

A few years ago, I spent some time helping in the nursery during Sunday school and church worship service. A four-year-old boy with brain damage could not resist the temptation to create some excitement by repeatedly grabbing another child's hair with both hands and pulling. The other child would scream; the teacher would rush over, quickly get the child released, and then scold the boy. The excitement was sudden and dramatic.

My job was to teach the boy not to do this. I tried punishment by sitting him in a chair in the corner, but then he cried and this caused more excitement. He was decisively unable to resist the temptation. So I consulted an expert at the Perkins School for the Blind, where Helen Keller's teacher was trained. She explained that the boy was stuck in repeating a pattern, and he needed a new one. Simply punishing him would not give him a new pattern. Instead I should just watch, and whenever I saw him being tempted I should gently take him by the elbow and lead him toward the blocks or another kind of play. I was to lead him in developing a new pattern. He could not do this himself; he needed gentle leadership. I tried this theory of patterning. The next Sunday, whenever I saw him start to develop that gleam in his eye as he was looking at another child, I gently took his elbow and led him toward some other toys. It worked beautifully; after two Sundays, the problem was solved.

That four-year-old boy was my son. He is now a college graduate with bachelor's and master's degrees in German, including a year's successful study of linguistics at Columbia University, plus a certificate in translation from the University of Mainz in Germany. He translates theological books and articles from German to English for graduate students and faculty researchers, and for publication. He has definitely learned some new patterns! But not without a little guidance and help.

I have also participated in a twelve-step group, Al-Anon, and have learned something about why twelve-step programs work. More than finding the willpower to just say no, they are about acknowledging that we do not have the power to free ourselves of temptation. They are about identifying the vicious cycles, the habitual patterns, that lead to addiction. Here are steps four and five: "We made a searching and fearless inventory of ourselves. We admitted to God, to ourselves, and to another human being the exact nature of our wrongs." We need to turn our lives over to God.

There is more. Step seven: "We humbly asked Him to remove our shortcomings." There is also guidance in making amends to people we have hurt (steps eight and nine). Additionally, the steps are about seeking "through prayer and meditation to improve our conscious contact with God as we understood Him, praying only for knowledge of His will for us and the power to carry that out" (step eleven). We need to focus on God's guidance to live a better life. We need help from others as well. We must confess our habits in a group, and ask others to help guide us to new life patterns. The shared laughter at our foibles in the group helps overcome a sense of isolation and shame, to share in developing new patterns. Helping each other develop those new patterns gives us friendship, community, and worthwhileness.

Throughout the Sermon on the Mount, Jesus helps us face our shortcomings realistically, but he does not simply focus on saying no to the temptations. He consistently emphasizes the new patterns, transforming initiatives, ways of deliverance. Here in Jesus' Prayer we pray for God to lead us not into temptation but to the way of deliverance. We will see more of this meaning in Chapter Seven.

One of the strengths of Jesus' Prayer is that each of us connects its petitions with basic struggles in our own life. It becomes personal and experiential for each of us, in unique ways. Whatever the reign of God means, it differs from much that happens in our own lives. Praying for the reign of God to come is praying for deliverance from where we lack justice, peace, healing, or joy, from where we miss the presence of God in our lives and in the world. Praying for daily needs to be met in our own and others' lives means praying for God's will to be done as it is not yet being done. I hope that the connections I have suggested help you make deeper and richer connections with the petitions of Jesus' Prayer in your own life, and in your own praying.

Remember that Jesus did not say only to pray these exact words, but to pray *like this*. Fill these words with connections in your own life. Fill these hopes with your own words. Pray for God's reign to come in a way that is not only in your own individual life, but in the lives of people all over the world whom God cares deeply for.

Investing in God's Reign and Restorative Justice

W e have seen that prayer is so central for Jesus that he gave us *two* parallel teachings on prayer in the Sermon on the Mount (Matt. 6:5–15). That is not all; he mentions prayer two other times, in Matthew 5:44 ("Pray for your persecutors") and 7:7–11 ("Ask, and it will be given to you . . .").

Justice is equally central for Jesus. The very next thing he does is give us a pair of parallel teachings on justice and money (Matt. 6:19–34). Nor is that all; he mentions justice for the poor in two other places (Matt. 5:42 and 6:2–4), both on giving to the poor. Thus prayer and justice receive a pair of main teachings and two additional ones. Clearly the Sermon on the Mount places major emphasis on prayer and economic justice.

Jesus' emphasis on economic justice is an important gospel for our world. Bread for the World reports that 1.2 billion people are trying to survive on less than a dollar a day.[1] An equally large number are struggling with deep poverty. Their children are often without school, sufficient food, medicine, and basic protection against common illnesses. I have seen this firsthand in Nicaragua, Brazil, Uganda, and Indonesia. Jesus' gospel of a God who cares for the poor is good news for the majority of the world. Indeed, the gospel is spreading most rapidly in India, Africa, and countries where there is extensive poverty. We have a gospel that is good news for the poor (Luke 4:18); it is also good news for the rich who get stuck in the vicious cycle of living for acquisition of ever more money instead of what matters in life.

The gospel calls all followers of Jesus to be part of a movement for justice for the poor—part of the gospel of good news for the poor. We have a highly relevant, life-and-death gospel for the real world that we live in.

PRACTICING RESTORATIVE JUSTICE AND LOYALTY TO GOD'S REIGN

Examining the two teachings in Matthew 6:19–34 together helps us see their meaning twice as clearly (Figure 7.1).

Traditional Righteousness: Don't Hoard Greedily

"Do not treasure up treasures on earth" is a pun in the Greek: the same Greek word is used twice, just as I have translated it. "Do not treasure up treasures on earth," or, "do not hoard hoards on earth." It warns against investing our efforts and income in riches for ourselves. It means basically the same thing as the parallel teaching, "You cannot serve God and mammon." *Mammon* is the Aramaic word for wealth or possessions. Anyone who is serving possessions or wealth is not serving God.

These are not teachings against making a living. They do not reject all possessions; they reject stinginess or greed (treasuring up treasures), hoarding the income for selfish pursuits rather than for serving God and the needs of others.

Greed as a sin is well known in most cultures, and most have traditional teachings warning against the foolishness of devoting one's life to getting rich (as, for example, in "You can't take it with you"). The Old Testament and Judaism have many sayings like this as well. The prophets warn repeatedly against greed. Jesus says, "Be on your guard against all kinds of greed, for one's life does not consist in the abundance of possessions" (Luke 12:15).

The Vicious Cycle: Serving Possessions While Claiming to Serve God

The vicious cycle in verse 19 is "moth and rust consume and thieves break in and steal." In verse 24, the vicious cycle is trying to serve both God and wealth; you "will either hate the one and love the other, or be devoted to the one and despise the other." Similarly, verse 25 warns of the vicious cycle of living in anxiety about what we will eat or wear.

What's vicious about this is not only that treasures of the sort we hoard here on earth waste away sooner or later, by rust, moths, or thievery. Ice cream is temporary too; we buy some and eat it, and it's gone. No surprise, no problem there; we expected it would be eaten and gone. We do not invest our hope for self-affirmation, worthiness, or meaningfulness in the ice cream. Nor do we hoard it in the hope it will last for years. Jesus never teaches, "Do not invest your treasures in ice cream, because it melts!" (Or, in Palestinian terms, "do not invest your treasures in falafel, because it molds.")

The foolishness of treasuring up treasures comes when I invest treasures with the expectation that they will give me a sense of life fulfillment, of being a worthy person, of being respected and appreciated by somebody important in my imagination or memory who did not give me love and appreciation when I really needed it. The problem is that I try to make my stamp in life, my lasting reputation, by giving myself over to accumulating possessions. Or I try to fill the hole in my life with consumer items. I endow money gathering with more drive and compulsion to prove myself worthwhile than it can really offer.

Acting greedily and not respecting God rightly distort our vision and result in foolishness. Isaiah 32:1–6 speaks of the deliverance that God will bring when rulers rule with justice, and "the eyes of those who have sight will not be closed." Then people will no longer call fools noble, and people who now are rash will have good judgment: "For fools . . . plot iniquity, to utter error concerning the Lord, to leave the craving of the

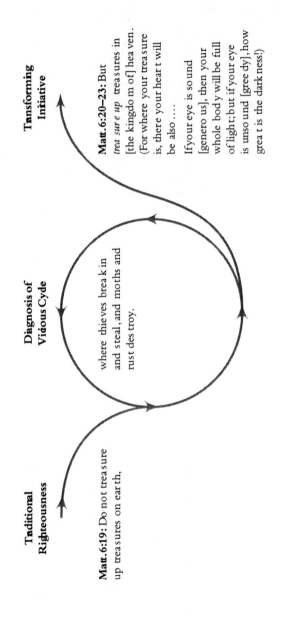

**Traditional
Righteousness**

Matt. 6:19: Do not treasure up treasures on earth,

**Diagnosis of
Vicious Cycle**

where thieves break in and steal, and moths and rust destroy.

**Transforming
Initiative**

Matt. 6:20–23: But *treasure up* treasures in [the kingdom of] heaven. (For where your treasure is, there your heart will be also. . . .

If your eye is sound [generous], then your whole body will be full of light; but if your eye is unsound [greedy], how great is the darkness!)

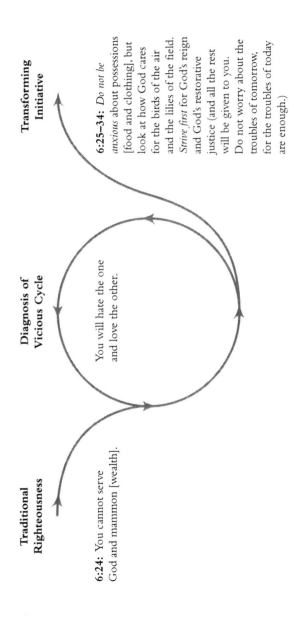

Traditional Righteousness

6:24: You cannot serve God and mammon [wealth].

Diagnosis of Vicious Cycle

You will hate the one and love the other.

Transforming Initiative

6:25–34: *Do not be anxious* about possessions [food and clothing], but look at how God cares for the birds of the air and the lilies of the field. *Strive first* for God's reign and God's restorative justice (and all the rest will be given to you. Do not worry about the troubles of tomorrow, for the troubles of today are enough.)

Figure 7.1. Practices of Investing in God's Reign and Justice.

hungry unsatisfied." Notice how foolishness is connected with
having a wrong relation with the Lord and with not seeing
clearly or doing justice for the hungry. But once deliverance
comes, a spirit from on high will be poured out on us, justice
will dwell in the wilderness, and the effect of restorative justice
will be peace (Isa. 32:15–17). Every time Jesus teaches about
foolishness, it is about someone looking to the wrong source in
a drive for worthiness, self-righteousness, honor, or reputation.
In Luke 12:15–21, Jesus says: "Take care! Be on your guard
against all kinds of greed; for one's life does not consist in the
abundance of possessions." Then he tells a parable:

> The land of a rich man produced abundantly. And he thought
> to himself, "What should I do, for I have no place to store my
> crops?" Then he said, "I will do this: I will pull down my
> barns and build larger ones, and there I will store all my grain
> and my goods. And I will say to my soul, "Soul, you have
> ample goods laid up for many years; relax, eat, drink, be
> merry." But God said to him, "You fool! This very night your
> life is being demanded of you. And the things you have pre-
> pared, whose will they be?" So it is with those who store up
> treasures for themselves but are not rich toward God.

Notice that the problem Jesus identifies is greed, failure to care
about the needs of others, believing that the fulfillment of life
depends on how much one owns. The rich fool's whole speech
is about *I, I, I, I* six times, and *my* four times; the one time he
says *you* he is talking to himself, not to others or to God ("Soul,
you have ample goods . . ."). The jolt comes when God enters
into the conversation. The rich fool does not expect that; he
thinks he is the only one in the conversation, the only one concerned about all his food and possessions. He eliminates others
from the ethical conversation about what to do with possessions. His foolishness comes from greedy selfishness, where
there should be a practice of justice toward others and respect
toward God.

Notice also the theme of gratitude versus ingratitude. What he thanks for producing the wealth is "the land," and in biblical understanding the land is a loan from God and still belongs to God. Those of us who have some wealth have it not only because of our own work but also because of the gift of natural resources; workers who have been brought up by their families and the society and customers have the wherewithal to purchase because of the society's just distribution of income; and the society's trust, justice, honesty, and peace. If we were transported to Nigeria, Nicaragua, Burma, or Russia, it would not be so easy. We have much to be grateful for. It is not merely about me, myself, and I. Where Matthew 6:20 speaks of storing up treasures in heaven, Luke 12:21 speaks of being "rich toward God." As we have seen, "heaven" in the Jewish worldview of Matthew is a respectful way of speaking obediently and respectfully about God and God's reign.

Matthew has three other teachings about foolishness. In 7:26 he says the foolish man who hears Jesus' words and does not do them is "like a foolish man who built his house on sand." In 15:14, Jesus calls the Pharisees "blind guides of the blind" when they teach people to take the money they had set aside for their elderly parents and give it instead to the temple authorities. Matthew 23:17 speaks of "blind fools," as we noticed when we were thinking about oaths and truth telling. It also has a dimension of greed in the fools' statement that the gold of the sanctuary is greater than the sanctuary (and God). It definitely is about misusing the name of God, not respecting God, while taking an oath we do not intend to fulfill. Jesus consistently diagnoses greed as causing blindness and distorted vision, foolishness and distorted thinking, dishonesty and a distorted relation with God. The evil eye in the Hebrew Bible and Judaism means the stingy, jealous, or greedy eye; the good, healthy, or sincere eye means the generous eye. For example, in Matthew 20:15, Jesus' parable of the generous employer says, "Or are you envious because I am generous?" (NRSV). Literally, the Greek says, "Or is your eye evil [stingy] because I am good?"

This is why Jesus often talks about blind guides. They fail to see, not through their physical eyes but with their heart; they invest their lives, drive, and purpose such that their heart is twisted and their perceptions distorted. Remember that Jesus taught about integrity of heart, which means consistently serving God with our whole selves. Investing our heart in possessions is idolatry, for where our investment goes there our heart goes also.

Transformation and Deliverance: Investing in God's Reign and Justice

Investing in heaven—storing up for ourselves treasures in heaven (verse 20)—does not mean buying our way into eternal life. Jesus warns, "It will be hard for a rich person to enter the kingdom of heaven" (Matt. 19:24). Heaven is "the sphere of God's rule where his will is done. . . . To have one's treasure in heaven" means to submit oneself "to God's sovereign rule."[2] The contrast is not this life and the life after, but this life, where there is injustice, and life transformed by God's reign.

The parallel teaching in verse 33 makes it clear: "Strive first for the kingdom of God and God's righteousness," which I have translated as "Strive first for God's reign and God's restorative justice." Jesus' teaching of the kingdom of God always cites Isaiah, where the seven characteristics of the kingdom of God are redemption, justice, peace, God's presence, joy over participation in what God is doing, healing, and repentance and return to God. Investing in God's reign and restorative justice means investing in where God is bringing these characteristics of the kingdom to occur. It means "a call for the total commitment of one's person in discipleship" and "the call for total allegiance."[3] "Strive first for God's reign and God's restorative justice" does not mean first this and then something else, it means "above all else." God wants your heart, not only your money; but Jesus is a realist—your heart tends to follow your money.

We know the reality: if we invest all our money in an expensive and luxurious car, then a significant amount of our caring and attention will go to how the car is doing. This is what is meant by our heart following our possessions. If, on the other hand, we invest our money in education and evangelism; prevention of HIV/AIDS, hunger, and poverty; in orphanages in poor countries, and agricultural development and teaching the gospel there, then we will pay more attention to how people we have given to are doing and how U.S. policies affect their lives. What Jesus is teaching about investment, heart, and a way of seeing reflects reality.

Jesus' transforming initiative is realistic: invest it in God's reign, in justice and charity, and your heart will be invested there as well.

Ronald Sider has written two thoughtful and balanced books on how to overcome much poverty. One is *Rich Christians in an Age of Hunger,* and the other is *Just Generosity: A New Vision for Overcoming Poverty in America.*[4] He and his family have lived among the poor for thirty years, in North Philadelphia and in Germantown, Philadelphia. They live a frugal life, investing much of their income in God's reign and justice, just as Jesus teaches. Consequently, Sider can write with compassion and dedication and does not need to explain away Jesus' teachings. I believe he illustrates what Jesus says: "Where your treasure is, there will your heart be also," and "If your eye is healthy [generous], your whole body will be full of light."

At the time of this writing, thirty-eight million Americans are attempting to get by on less than the official income level that designates them as living in poverty. The number has been steadily increasing for the last five years. Sider shows that the rich are getting richer and the poor poorer, with the situation worsening in the last few years.

Some argue that this is caused by governmental policies, and the solution requires a change in governmental policies to do justice for the poor. Others argue that the poor cause their own poverty and need to build character and responsibility. Sider makes very clear what almost anyone who works with the poor knows: both are true. It is a distraction to argue as if either position has all the truth and the other holds none. Furthermore, they interact: unjust policies and resulting conditions of hopelessness cause great discouragement and therefore undermine hope and character. We blame the poor for lack of self-discipline and then refuse to invest money in education, jobs, and a living wage for them. This is exactly what "vicious cycle" means. Sider then works out the kind of change needed for a new vision for overcoming poverty. It requires a living wage for the working poor, adequate investment in education, and increasing work on the part of churches to deepen the faith, moral character, and hope of poor people so they can benefit from what opportunities are there. All have to work together.

The important point here is that Sider can see the situation clearly because he has not invested his own income in hoarding treasures for himself, but in involving himself in faith-based programs to help the poor make a living. He is an example that shows Jesus is right: investing our money in God's reign and justice does give us a clearer vision—and a sense of the action we need to take to participate in alleviating poverty and bringing that reign into being.

Sider identifies some truly impressive church programs doing much that is dramatically hopeful. For example, in Good Samaritan Ministries in Ottawa County, Michigan, a "relational ministry team" of five to seven people from one of the churches is matched with each poor family. They are trained in how to provide "a mixture of love, regular contact and emotional support, prayer, and individualized care that government agencies cannot provide." The ministry team offers "help in finding an apartment, untangling legal problems, fixing or finding a car, emergency food and clothing, finding a job, improving work skills . . . budgeting, getting out of debt, financial planning," and most important, friendship. They do not impose their faith;

"they freely share their faith and talk about the way that God can transform a person's values, character, and life." The result: "Ottawa County became the first county in America to put every able-bodied welfare recipient in a job."[5]

Ron Sider and Heidi Rolland Unruh have also published *Churches That Make a Difference,* a book full of descriptions of churches that are making a difference for these concerns.[6]

Some people advocate that the government should stop aiding the poor; instead, they say, we should rely on churches to do that. They speak as though they are expressing loyalty to the churches, but Sider points out that the Bible repeatedly declares the obligation of the king (the government in the time of the prophets) to do justice to the poor. Jesus repeatedly criticized the Jerusalem authorities (the local government then) for their greed and injustice to the poor. Sider sees clearly what almost everyone knows who works in church-based programs: the need is far too great for it all to be dumped on the back of churches. Church mentoring programs such as Good Samaritan Ministries are fairly new and small; they cannot meet all the need, and their way of meeting what need they can depends on government assistance where it is crucial. Might those who do not see this practical truth be short-sighted because their heart is too wrapped up in their own treasures?

GOD CARES FOR THE CREATION

What about Jesus' teaching that God cares for the birds, the lilies, and us?

> Look at the birds of the air; they neither sow nor reap nor gather into barns, and yet your heavenly Father feeds them. Are you not of more value than they? And can any of you by worrying add a single hour to your span of life? And why do you worry about clothing? Consider the lilies of the field,

how they grow; they neither toil nor spin, yet I tell you, even Solomon in all his glory was not clothed like one of these. But if God so clothes the grass of the field, which is alive today and tomorrow is thrown into the oven, will he not much more clothe you—you of little faith? Therefore do not worry, saying, "What will we eat?" or "What will we drink?" or "What will we wear?" For it is the Gentiles who strive for all these things; and indeed your heavenly Father knows that you need all these things. But strive first for the kingdom of God and his righteousness, and all these things will be given you as well [Matt. 6:26–33].

Some people have heard this as instruction not to make any effort, but instead just lie back and let God take care of us. That misses Jesus' point. It is not about our passivity, but about God's activity. Jesus' emphasis in the climaxes of the Sermon on the Mount is that God is actively present, caring for all with compassion and sensitivity. In the climax of the fifth chapter, he points out that God is active in nature, giving sunshine and rain to the just and unjust alike. In the teachings about almsgiving, praying, and fasting, Jesus says again and again that God is present, seeing in secret and knowing what we need even before we ask for it. In Jesus' Prayer, Jesus indicates that God is actively present, giving us our daily needs, forgiving us, and delivering us from evil. In the climax of the teaching in Matthew 7:7–11, Jesus teaches that God hears our prayers and "will give good things to those who ask him." Here in 6:26–33, Jesus is consistent with those other messages. He says as clearly as can be done that God is actively involved in nature, caring for creation. His point is not that we should do nothing; it is that God is present, caring, and actively providing.

In each of these teachings, Jesus names practical action that his followers take. We participate in what God is doing. We love our enemies as God loves God's enemies. We give aid to the poor and pray and fast in private. We forgive others as God forgives us. We do unto others as we want others to do for us, just as God gives us good gifts. We strive first for God's reign and restorative justice just as God is caring for creation, including the birds, the lilies, and us. It is never about doing nothing, but always about participating in these caring actions of God's.

Larry Rasmussen wrote *Earth Community Earth Ethics,* an award-winning book that argues we will never get our relation to God's creation right until we see that God is deeply involved in caring for it. Too often we think of "nature" as something outside of us, something "over there," distant from us, that we can use as we want. Only when we see that God is deeply involved in caring for creation, and likewise deeply involved in caring for us, and that we are part of creation and it is part of us, will we begin to treat it with respect and healing rather than manipulation and destruction.[7]

Rasmussen says exactly what Jesus says: God is actively caring even for the little birds and the lilies in the field, and God is caring for us. We are with the birds and the flowers, part of God's community of care. We are now seeing that our greedy consumption of God's one-time gift of oil, natural gas, and coal is causing it all to be used up so that future generations will no longer have those resources to keep them warm. Our greedy consumption is causing the polar ice caps to melt, the Gulf of Mexico to warm up, hurricanes to be more intense than ever in history, chemical pollution to cause unexplained illnesses, and great future disasters that we cannot yet even imagine. Jesus is right about greed: what we do to the creation we do to what God deeply cares about—and we do it to God's creation, which is essential for our own healthy survival.

WILLIAM FAULKNER, "THE BEAR"

I have a special sense of identification with William Faulkner for a peculiarly personal reason: he used to come watch me practice running the high hurdles at the University of Virginia every afternoon. Maybe this fit his poetic and tragic sense: many of his stories are about imperfect humans trying to surmount difficult obstacles, and not always succeeding. He was shy, as I was shy, but together we expressed respect for the beauty of God's creation on those wonderful spring days in Charlottesville. I have a deeper sense of gratitude for Faulkner's sensitivity to human nature, and to God's nature, in his writing than I can put in words.

I especially identify with his story "The Bear." In the tale, a teenage Ike McCaslin is taught by Sam Fathers to hunt in the Mississippi wilderness. The way Faulkner tells it, readers are invited to identify with Ike, to go with him as he becomes part of the wilderness; we thereby become part of the wilderness with him.

We and Ike learn a religious devotion to God's creation: Ike first has to serve "his apprenticeship in the woods which would prove him worthy to be a hunter. . . . He entered his novitiate to the true wilderness with Sam beside him. . . ."

Yet Faulkner hints at a foreboding problem: the wilderness faces destruction by men and machines that regularly gnaw at its edges.

Waiting silently in his appointed stand in the woods, Ike knows from the woodpecker's sudden silence that Old Ben the bear has come to look at him, although Ben does not allow Ike to have a look at him. Ike knows that Sam is right: the only way the bear will allow himself to be seen is if Ike becomes more a part of the woods—leaves his mechanical intrusion behind— and comes without his gun. "It's the gun. . . . You will have to choose," Sam says.

Ike leaves the next morning before light, without breakfast and without his gun, with only a compass and a stick for the snakes. But he still cannot find the bear. So "he relinquished completely" to the wilderness. He leaves his watch and compass with his stick and enters the wilderness (meaning not just that he goes into the wilderness—he is already there—but that he enters it by truly becoming a part of it). He becomes so much a part of the wilderness that he learns how to find his way when lost without the compass, doubling back on his own trail in wide circles so as to find his way to where he began. Then he sees the fresh footprint of a bear in the wet, swampy ground, filling with water. He follows the disappearing footprints just fast enough to keep up with them before they vanish in the water seeping into them. Once he becomes thoroughly part of the wilderness, he sees the bear, and the bear stands looking at him. He was thoroughly at home, identified, himself a part of the woods.

But they did not have the dog strong enough and fearless enough to hold the bear at bay long enough for the hunters to arrive. Then Boon Hogganbeck, part Chickasaw, part white, and part black, trained a powerful wild dog he named Lion, made him his dog, and developed powerful loyalty to Lion. Although Boon could hit neither bear nor man nor squirrel with a gun, he was strong and fearless. Finally in the next year's hunt, Lion bayed the bear, charged him, and caught him by the throat, but the bear grabbed Lion and raked his belly with his forepaws. Boon, deeply faithful to Lion, suddenly rushed the bear, locked his legs around the bear's belly from behind, with his left hand under the bear's throat, and stabbed him with his knife in his right hand, working and probing the buried blade. The bear fell, then stood up again, and Boon was still working and probing with the knife, and then the bear fell again, "of a piece, as a tree falls, so that all three of them, man, dog, and bear, seemed to bounce once." Boon, whose left ear was shredded, his left arm mauled, and his right boot ripped from knee to instep, immediately wrapped the dog in his coat. It took hours before they could get back to the camp where the doctor was. Wounded and bleeding though he was, "Boon would not let the doctor touch him until he had seen to Lion." Sadly, Lion did not recover; Boon buried him and stayed sitting at the grave for days, guarding it and mourning Lion's death.

Faulkner shows us Boon, caring for Lion, God's creation. He shows us Ike and the hunting party evidencing huge respect for the whole wilderness, as well as for Ben, the bear. Being in tune with the wilderness is for Ike a Christian initiation.

Yet Faulkner also shows possession of the land as a curse, because it has brought the ongoing curse of slavery. Possession of the land corrupts ongoing generations of Ike's family and leads to destruction of the wilderness by the attack of machines, a logging train, and commercialization—symbolizing the worldwide attack on the creation by the power of humanmade machines. Ike says it is not his grandfather's, father's, or his land to possess. It is God's.

Ike, who is the sole remaining member of his family, vows to relinquish the land as he has relinquished his gun. I think this means he intends to distribute it among the descendants of the slaves who worked it and made it profitable, who made it possible to build the big homes and pass it on. It is clear that he wants to end the exploitation of the land and the slaves for selfish profit.

Yet in the end Ike fails to carry through on his vow. Just as we are failing to carry through on God's command to care for the creation.

Faulkner has led us to see ourselves as part of nature, as Rasmussen says biblical people must; he also leads us to personal awareness of the tragic heritage of slavery and racism. Part of Faulkner's greatness is his tragic honesty, leading us to enter into a deep and realistic sense of this shame and guilt and how it has shaped us, even unknowingly. He brings it out into the open where we can deal with it and let some healing do its work. In "The Bear," he interweaves that with our heritage of destroying the earth.

While Faulkner was at the University of Virginia in 1957 and 1958, a student asked him whether Ike's renunciation of his inheritance was the action of a moral hero. Faulkner's answer fit his realism about human nature: "Well, there are some people in any time and age that cannot face and cope with the problems." There are three kinds of people, he said:

The first says, This is rotten, I'll have no part of it, I will take death first. The second says, This is rotten, I don't like it, I can't do anything about it, but at least I will not participate in it myself, I will go off into a cave or climb a pillar to sit on. The third says, This stinks and I'm going to do something about it. [Ike] McCaslin is the second. He says, This is bad, and I will withdraw from it. What we need are people who will say, This is bad and I'm going to do something about it, I'm going to change it.[8]

YOUR HEART WILL BE
WHERE YOUR TREASURE IS

Too many of us who care about the creation have been like Ike. We renounce using too much plastic; we monitor usage of gasoline, electricity, and natural gas. But we do not devise and support policies that truly espouse conservation beyond our own individual renunciation. We need realistic people who will say, "This is bad and I'm going to do something effective about it; I'm going to change it."

Jesus is a realist. He does not say, "Keep investing your life in piling up possessions, but at the same time keep your heart pure and well intentioned." He says, "Change where you are making your investments. Invest them in God's reign and restorative justice." Because people's hearts and perceptions follow their money, should there not be financial consequences for consuming large quantities of energy and nonrenewable resources?

Do we need more realistic Ike McCaslins, imperfect people who will not merely relinquish their lifestyle of lavish consumption but also persuade the rest of us to do something to change the greedy consumption that is destroying God's good creation? If they follow Jesus' realism—that the heart follows investment—will they help us move toward changing the financial incentives that govern consumption? Will these realists ask, "Since consuming oil has huge costs for people all over the world, should the financial incentives be changed so that consumption of oil is discouraged and public transportation is encouraged?" Or if a more sensible, problem-solving kind of person emerges, one who knows what Jesus says is true—that our heart and our perception are transformed according to where our financial interests are—how will this person urge us to change our habits, lifestyles, and policies? Who among us will step forward to participate in making this way of grace and deliverance a reality in our society?

The need to change financial incentives toward conservation and away from gluttony is truly urgent. In his *Earth Community Earth Ethics,* Larry Rasmussen writes that until the coming of industrial society, we consumed only renewable resources. But now we use up energy stored millions of years ago in oil, natural gas, and coal to power our machines that use up the earth's resources to an extent that is rapidly destroying the very earth we depend on for our lives. Each day the industrialized economy consumes "an amount of energy the planet required 10,000 days to create."[9] At that rate, the limited amount that exists is being used up fast. And China, India, and other nations are rapidly gearing up to do as we do—devouring the earth all the faster. It means we are headed for a global crash with increasing speed.

No other animal has attacked the earth as humans are now doing. No other humans in all of human history have destroyed earth as our energy-driven machines are now doing. Something entirely unprecedented is happening in recent years, and we are letting it happen as if it were all natural. But it is destroying all that is natural. When the earth is destroyed, all that is natural on it, including the human part of nature, is threatened with extinction. Human-made machines are now by far the biggest part of nature, and they are destroying the system as surely as a rapidly growing cancer destroys a human body.

Rasmussen points out that the United States used four hundred *m*illion metric tons of industrial materials in 1950, and by

1993, just forty-three years later, it was using four and a half *bil-lion* tons. That is over a thousand-fold increase in that short time. When China and India and Indonesia and other nations follow in that course, the world will literally be used up. Before that, the world may be at world war over the scarcities with nuclear weapons.

Unless we take Jesus seriously: God actively cares for the birds and animals, and for the flowers and the vegetables, and for the humans who depend on God's caring for the creation in order to live. So we need to be part of God's caring. And where our financial incentives are, there our hearts will follow, and our eyes are motivated to see what our hearts care about. So, realistically, we must change the financial incentives so conservation replaces consumption. In a hurry.

8

Forgoing Judgment
for Forgiveness

I n Matthew 7, why does Jesus say, "Do not judge"? Does he
mean we should make no ethical judgments about right and
wrong? Surely not. In the first three Gospels, Jesus confronted the powers and authorities of Jerusalem for their injustice thirty-seven times. Even so, they refused to repent and
change. Instead, they plotted to have him crucified. Jesus clearly
made ethical judgments about the injustice of the authorities.
What he opposes is the judgmental and authoritarian culture
symbolized by the Pharisees, who were judging others in the
sense of condemning them. So when we look at the transfor-
mational message in this passage of Matthew, we see the perspective of Figure 8.1.

JUDGMENT AND FORGIVENESS

Here, as elsewhere, Jesus teaches a restorative justice that goes
beyond what the Pharisees do in their fastidious practice of excluding whoever and whatever is impure. His teachings do not
condemn nonconformists but instead restore outcasts to community. Far from imposing an authoritarian tradition on everyone who appears to be out of step with the authorities, this kind
of justice encourages practices that produce mutual help in
community, helping others follow Jesus in their lives.

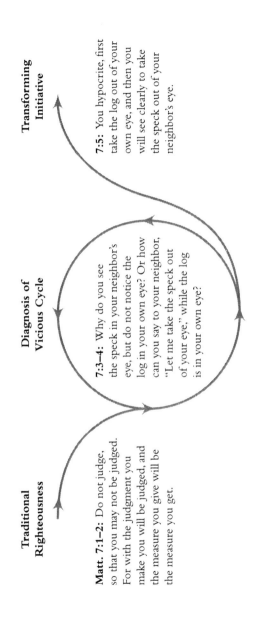

Traditional Righteousness

Matt. 7:1–2: Do not judge, so that you may not be judged. For with the judgment you make you will be judged, and the measure you give will be the measure you get.

Diagnosis of Vicious Cycle

7:3–4: Why do you see the speck in your neighbor's eye, but do not notice the log in your own eye? Or how can you say to your neighbor, "Let me take the speck out of your eye," while the log is in your own eye?

Transforming Initiative

7:5: You hypocrite, first take the log out of your own eye, and then you will see clearly to take the speck out of your neighbor's eye.

Figure 8.1. Practices of Forgoing Judgmentalism and Learning from Errors.

Traditional Righteousness: Do Not Judge

Jesus' command not to condemn others as though you were in a position to judge as only God can do connects directly with the theme of forgiveness in Jesus' Prayer. Condemning others closes them out of the community of love. It refuses to forgive them for what they do that you disagree with. It considers them to be unredeemable; basically it damns them. Jesus means, "Do not condemn others and do not refuse to forgive them."

God alone is the ultimate judge. "Lest you be judged" probably points to God's future judgment when the kingdom will come in its fullness. Judging someone else sets me over that person, as if I were God. God says "my ways are higher than your ways and my thoughts than your thoughts" (Isa. 55:9). I have no right to condemn another person—as if my thoughts were as high as God's thoughts.

Jesus is absolutely clear about the central importance of forgiveness in his prayer: we pray to our Father in heaven to "forgive us our debts, as we also have forgiven our debtors." *Debts* translates to a word in Aramaic that means both sins and economic debts. Matthew wrote for Jews who knew this Aramaic background, but Luke (11:4) wrote for Greeks who did not understand Aramaic, so he used the word that clearly means "sins" and then added "indebted," thus making both meanings clear: "Forgive us our *sins,* for we ourselves forgive everyone *indebted* to us."

Jesus' Prayer makes clear that everyone has sins in need of forgiving. Then, to be really clear, Matthew 6:14–15 adds an explanation: "For if you forgive others their transgressions, your heavenly Father will also forgive you; but if you do not forgive others, neither will your Father forgive your transgressions." (*Transgressions* here means misdeeds against other people and against God.) Some people are surprised that Jesus really said that. They are used to believing in "cheap forgiveness"—God forgives us freely, without obligation. But God's way is in fact a way of deliverance; we participate in it by forgiving others. By forgiving others we receive God's forgiveness and let it transform us into being humble, repentant, and grateful enough to show forgiveness toward others.

God wants to embrace us, as the father runs and embraces the Prodigal Son (Luke 15:11–32). But we do not receive, participate in, or return the embrace unless we really live it, participating in it by sharing God's forgiveness in our way of relating to others. This is why the father of the Prodigal Son urges the elder brother to rejoice that his sibling has returned.

Jesus makes this clear again in Matthew 18:21–35. Peter asks him how often he should forgive someone who sins against him, and he answers, "Not seven times, but, I tell you, seventy-seven times." Then Jesus tells his parable about a king who forgave his slave an enormous debt—the equivalent of about two hundred thousand years' wages—but then the forgiven slave turned around and refused to forgive a fellow slave who owed him only one hundred days' wages. When the king heard about this, he was outraged, and said: "Should you not have had mercy on your fellow slave, as I had mercy on you?" He handed the unforgiving slave over to be tortured until he could repay his enormous debt—which was clearly impossible in his lifetime. Jesus concludes: "So my heavenly Father will also do to every one of you, if you do not forgive your brother or sister from your heart."

Why does Jesus confront us ("If you do not forgive others, neither will your Father forgive your transgressions")? He does not mean that we can earn God's forgiveness by forgiving others. Our acts of forgiveness are not the measure of God's forgiveness of us. Just the opposite: God's merciful forgiving is the measure by which we are to forgive others, mercifully and more fully than we think we can. God's forgiveness is so much greater than ours because God sees all that we do or think, all of who we are, even what we are sure is hidden. This call to forgiveness transcends making light of the wrong that others do. It concerns knowing that all of us sin much more than others see and even more than we ourselves admit. Because God knows fully how much we sin, when God forgives us it goes much farther and deeper than our forgiving does. As the Apostle Paul says, "There

is no one who is righteous, not even one" (Rom. 3:10). Therefore the measure for our forgiveness is God's merciful forgiving.
Because God really knows our inner heart, the forgiveness we
give to others is more than simply forgiving a specific hurtful
action; it is accepting the other person as having secret sins far
more than we know, just as God accepts ours.

Luke 6:27–38 gives us the same teaching from Jesus. There
Jesus teaches directly, "Do not condemn, and you will not be
condemned. Forgive, and you will be forgiven." This connects
Jesus' teaching about not judging with his teaching about forgiving others, just as we saw in connecting Matthew 7:1–5 with
the prayer for forgiveness in Jesus' Prayer. Furthermore, where
Matthew uses the general Greek word *krino,* to judge, Luke uses
the specific word *katadikazo,* to condemn. This confirms that
"Do not judge" means "Do not condemn." Luke also connects
"Forgive" and "Do not judge" with "Love your enemies." As
New Testament scholar David Garland says, "The real danger of
a judgmental spirit is not simply that one will get back what one
dishes out to others, but that it strangles the love for the other."[1]

Howard Rees, a beloved minister to students in the universities of Washington, D.C., embodied the rule that if you are not
able to say something good about someone else, practice quietness. He was a master at finding something good in others to
praise and encourage. Not surprisingly, his ministry blossomed
beautifully. He incarnated the mercy, humility, love, and toler-
ance that Jesus is calling for. Students appreciated it and felt encouraged to model themselves after Rees. I am one of those
grateful students.

The Vicious Cycle: Ignoring
My Own Deficits as I Judge Others

Why does Jesus talk about having a log in our eye? I think it is
because he has a sense of humor and wants us to laugh at ourselves, so we can break through our defensiveness against admit-
ting our own errors.

We have all experienced getting a speck or a piece of dirt in our eye. This must have been especially true for Jesus, a carpenter. Here, a speck means a small sin. Jesus asks me to laugh at my own tendency to notice small faults in others while blind to my own faults.

Dale Allison and John Stott, authors of studies of Matthew and the Sermon on the Mount, put it insightfully. "Human beings unhappily possess an inbred proclivity," Allison says, "to mix ignorance of themselves with arrogance toward others. . . ." Stott adds, "We have a fatal tendency to exaggerate the faults of others and minimize the gravity of our own. We seem to find it impossible, when comparing ourselves with others, to be strictly objective and impartial."[2]

Why does Jesus focus on our eyes, our seeing, so often? He often speaks of our not seeing what is happening, of our being blind to the truth that is dawning. Several of his healings involve the blind receiving their sight. In the Sermon on the Mount, he teaches about the eye being distorted by lusting for a woman and greed for possessions (Matt. 5:28–29, 6:22–23). Here in this teaching about the speck and the log he says "your own eye" three times, which points to vision distorted by our desire to make excuses for ourselves, to be defensive and justify what we have done. Jesus clearly teaches that our loyalties and interests, our investment and the objects of our greed and coveting distort our way of seeing. His way is an ethics not only of rules but of self-awareness—awareness of our foibles and our tendency to distort what we see. We do not see objectively; we see through the fog of our own self-justification.

The Apostle Paul knew about the fog of self-justification. He began his Letter to the Romans by naming sins that Jews blamed Greeks for: they failed to honor God or give God thanks; their philosophers claimed to be wise yet recommended homosexual practices, which they themselves engaged in; and they were filled with vices of hostility rather than peace—envy, murder, strife, deceit, craftiness, gossip, slander, God hating, insolence, arrogance, and boasting (Rom. 1:18–32). We can imagine that in

writing this way Paul succeeded in getting Jews to nod know-
ingly and feel superior, just as Amos had his fellow Israelites
cheering as he named sins of their enemies (Amos 1–2). But
then, like Amos, Paul turned the tables on his fellow Jews:
"Therefore you have no excuse, whoever you are, when you
judge others, for in passing judgment on another you condemn
yourself, because you, the judge, are doing the very same things"
(Rom. 2:1).

Paul then named the idolatry that many of his fellow Jews
could be blamed for: believing in their own self-righteousness
rather than in God's grace, and therefore becoming filled with
vices of deceit, hostile speech, cursing, bitterness, violence, and
not knowing the way of peace or the fear of God (Rom. 3:
10–18).

Paul concluded that none of us has a right to judge others.
Nor are we even able to, because our judgment is so clouded by
our own folly and self-justification (the log we all have in our
own eye): "All, both Jews and Greeks, are under the power of
sin" (Rom. 3:9). Then he moved to forgiveness: "Since all have
sinned and fall short of the glory of God; they are now justified
by his grace as a gift, through the redemption that is in Christ
Jesus. . . ." None of us has grounds for boasting and judging; we
all depend on God's forgiveness given to us in Jesus Christ
(Rom. 3:27).

Paul's letter to the Romans is organized such that each early
chapter reaches its climax in one of the later chapters. The section that climaxes this early teaching against judging is Romans
14:1–15:13: "Why do you pass judgment on your brother or
sister? Or you, why do you despise your brother or sister? For
we will all stand before the judgment seat of God. . . . Let us
therefore no longer pass judgment on one another. . . . For the
kingdom of God is not [judging others about] food and drink
but righteousness and peace and joy in the Holy Spirit. . . . Let
us then pursue what makes for peace and for mutual upbuild-
ing. . . . Welcome one another, just as Christ has welcomed you."

Here, Paul carries out what Jesus teaches: confess and acknowledge your own sins, and make changes in your life that remove the log in your own eye. He is powerfully urging Christians not to be the judging and condemning kind who spread hostility, arrogance, boasting, slander, bitterness, and violence, rather than Jesus' way of peace. Instead we are to be the mutually forgiving kind who base our actions on the way of forgiveness, grace, confession of our own sins, and deliverance in Christ Jesus.

Transformation and Deliverance: Repent and Help Each Other

When he says, "Take the log out of your eye," Jesus is calling for repentance—acknowledging our own need for change, and actually making the change. The way of repentance is central to Jesus' announcement that the reign of God is at hand: God is present, graciously delivering us; repent and believe the good news. When we repent and allow Jesus to loosen our defensiveness, stop hiding our real selves from others, admit that we have a problem, and allow God's grace to bring about a turning in our lives, that is participating in grace. The reign of God then breaks into our lives. When we allow Jesus to convert our judging into openness and gratitude, it really is the grace of God breaking into our shame.

Transformation and deliverance correct the vicious cycle of self-righteousness by grace. Grace teaches peacemaking, not putting all the blame on others and building up hostility against them but acknowledging our own contribution to the problem. Acknowledging that I have a log in my own eye, that I need forgiveness, and that I must forgive others is one more practice of the just peacemaking ethic that we looked at in Chapter Five.[3]

This kind of peacemaking practice began with Dietrich Bonhoeffer. He had the opportunity to leave Germany and become a professor in the United States, and thus avoid the threat of death that hung over him. But he decided he needed to acknowledge his part in Germany's guilt for its support of Hitler. He returned to Germany to lead churches in opposing the Reich. He was imprisoned and eventually executed, but first he led others in making a courageous witness, leading some Jews to safety in Switzerland, and writing an acknowledgment of the guilt of Germany's defection from Christ. The confession of guilt is remarkable, coming from the person who arguably did the most to oppose the evil and who, one would think, had the least cause for guilt.[4]

Bonhoeffer wrote that this confession can be made only by the miracle and the grace "by which Christ holds fast the fallen and preserves community with them" in the church. It is not the confession of individual misdeeds by comparison with the misdeeds of others, but confession of guilt toward Christ who has taken our guilt upon himself and freed us from its burden. "I am guilty," he wrote, "of cowardly silence when I should have spoken. I am guilty of untruthfulness and hypocrisy in the face of threatening violence. I am guilty of disowning without mercy the poorest of my neighbors. I am guilty of disloyalty and falling away from Christ." He confesses at length the guilt of the church for not speaking clearly, for not opposing the idolatry, for being sucked up into the ideology of the powerful: "The church confesses that it has witnessed the arbitrary use of brutal force, the suffering in body and soul of countless innocent people, that it has witnessed oppression, hatred, and murder without raising its voice for the victims and without finding ways of rushing to help them. It has become guilty of the lives of the weakest and most defenseless brothers and sisters of Jesus Christ." He then confesses the guilt of the nations that have failed to prevent this horrible guilt. The justification and renewal of the West, he believes, "lies completely in God's renewal of the church, which leads it into community with the resurrected and living Jesus Christ." This "can happen only in the restoration of justice, order, and peace in one way or another and then by the forgiveness of past guilt."[5]

After the war, Bonhoeffer's confession of guilt for himself, for other individuals, for the churches, and for nations became a movement among many German churches to repent and confess guilt, and to dedicate themselves to a truer following of Jesus. It was eventually taken up by President Richard von Weizsäcker and Chancellor Willy Brandt, when they publicly confessed Germany's sins. The world was amazed and impressed; there was scant precedent for leaders ever to confess their nations' sins. The movement has grown: the prime minister of Japan, the prime minister of Great Britain, Presidents George H. W. Bush and Bill Clinton, and others have acknowledged shortcomings that contributed to massacres and serious injustice. Acknowledging responsibility has greatly decreased bitterness and prevented subsequent outbreak of vengeful war. Repentance is for individuals, for churches, and even for nations.

Why does Jesus say "your brother" three times in Matthew 7:1–5? Why does Jesus conclude by saying that once you remove the log from your own eye you will see clearly enough to help your brother get the speck out of his? Is it irony, poking fun at our always wanting to correct someone else, with the implication that we should never try to correct someone else but concentrate instead on our own program? Some do interpret it that way, as only ironical. My criticism of someone else's shortcomings frequently reflects the same flaw in myself. The only correction needed is my own repentance, and the shortcoming I think I see in someone else will clear up automatically. Robert Guelich, a writer whom I respect greatly, interprets Jesus' teaching this way. He says it redirects attention from a false desire to correct a brother to the need for personal repentance. Jesus does not mean that if we take the beam out of our own eye then we really should take the speck out of our brother's eye. Rather, he intends to focus attention on our own self-correction. Nevertheless, Guelich concludes that Jesus' teaching does not preclude "the desire or the need to aid another who is in the wrong by humbly seeking out an awareness of one's own great failings and God's mercy to correct or discipline a brother."[6]

I believe that besides calling for repentance Jesus actually calls for help for "the brother." In the New Testament, "brother" usually means fellow community member, fellow follower of Jesus.[7] Healthy community requires the practice of forgiveness, and it also requires mutual, loving correction.

We have already noticed that Jesus confronts the powers and authorities of Jerusalem for their injustice thirty-seven times in the first three Gospels. Every reader of the Gospels knows that Jesus lovingly confronts others for their sins, seeking to lead them to repentance. He wants a community where we really do help each other with our biases. The help we give to our fellow disciples is based in forgiveness. It is the help of forgiveness, encouragement, and correction—all offered mutually—that we are to render to our fellow disciples. This is not judging; it is taking seriously the reality that everyone needs a few blunt friends to tell us the truth honestly and lovingly.

After all, Jesus gives clear instructions about what you are to do "if another member sins against you." Then "go and point out the fault when the two of you are alone. If the member listens to you, you have regained that one. But if you are not listened to, take one or two others along with you," and try again. If that does not work, try bringing it before the larger community (Matt. 18:15–20). The key is to go talk with the brother only after repenting oneself, and to do it in a spirit of love and mutual forgiveness.

TWO KINDS OF CHRISTIANITY: JUDGMENTAL AND MUTUALLY FORGIVING

In these teachings, Jesus clearly says: Do not be the kind of person who regularly condemns others, but the kind who regularly practices forgiveness and repentance. Jesus is talking to his disciples, the Christians, admonishing his followers not to condemn others but always to forgive them and make self-correction.

This suggests there are two kinds of Christians. Some Christians know they need forgiveness, so they pray Jesus' prayer sincerely ("Father, forgive us our sins as we forgive others who sin against us"). These are the mutual-forgiveness Christians; they know they need the Father's forgiveness, and they are forgiving toward others. Similarly, some Christians know they first need to acknowledge their own faults and errors before they can see clearly enough to help others acknowledge and deal with theirs. They know they need forgiveness and repentance.

Other Christians spend their time and energy judging people. They do not see the speck in their eye, let alone the log. They keep thinking others are in the wrong. They pray: "Father, forgive us our sins; we are better than others who are definitely sinners." These are judgmental Christians; they know others are sinners and in the wrong, and they believe their job is to censor so that others' sins do not infect them. These are Christians who relate to others in an unforgiving, judging, self-righteous way. Jesus warns us that the judgmental Christians who are not practicing forgiveness toward others are not themselves forgiven.

It may seem odd to call both types "Christian." We are used to calling the judgmental kind non-Christians. Surely, we say, the heart of Christian faith is that we are sinners ourselves, and that we live only by God's grace and forgiveness. If this is not true, what is Jesus' forgiveness from the cross about? What part of "Father, forgive them for they do not know what they are doing" do we not understand? What part of "There is none righteous, no, not one" do we not understand? What part of "If you do not forgive others, neither will your Father forgive your trespasses" do we not understand?

Anyone who does not live by forgiveness must have some other kind of religion and should not be called a Christian. But the assumption that we Christians are righteous and not judgmental is exactly the kind of judgmentalism that Jesus calls on us to repent from practicing. Assuming that sin belongs to others, to outsiders, not to members of a Christian group, is exactly what Jesus works to correct again and again. The Pharisees taught that corruption comes from outside—from Romans, or Gentiles, or tax collectors, or prostitutes, or lepers, or women. They taught that we faithful people have to practice exclusion when we meet together to eat; we must not associate with any of those outsiders because they do not observe laws concerning purity. As they say, only insiders who perform ritual washing from the impurity that comes from contact with outsiders and who tithe even the very smallest spices ("mint, dill, and cumin") can be allowed into the community that eats together. Because the Pharisees put all the blame for corruption on outsiders, it led to resentment, anger, judgmentalism, and rebellion against outsiders. This is why Jesus points out the log of violence in their eye again and again and even warns that it will lead to the temple being destroyed. When the rebellion against Rome did eventually boil up in 66 A.D., Rome came with its army, defeated the rebellion, destroyed the temple, killed thousands of Jews, razed Jerusalem, and exiled the Jews from the Promised Land.

The danger for Christians comes when we consider ourselves to be the people of forgiveness, and outsiders (non-Christians) to be the people who are judgmental. The truth is that many who claim the label "Christian" for themselves are in fact clearly judgmental. The world sees that. The world sees this judgmentalism so clearly that many think it is characteristic of all Christians. They think that what it means to be a Christian is to be judgmental, authoritarian, and self-righteous. We need to say clearly that we as Christians have a log in our own eye, and we need to repent for it.

Numerous sociological studies support the idea of two kinds of Christianity. The judging kind focuses energy on drawing boundaries that separate righteous Christians from those who are unrighteous by defining orthodox beliefs and having authorities impose those right beliefs on the inside community. This kind tends to have some fear about the precariousness of life and about not belonging to the insider group. Drawing boundaries helps insiders know they belong to the righteous community. Faith needs to be protected against external threat.

Order and decorum defend the sense of right order and belonging. Sociology of religion, and church history, show that this
judging kind of Christianity tends to go together with prejudice, racism, nationalism, and support for the death penalty and
for making war.

In contrast, the mutually forgiving kind of Christianity emphasizes prayer, following Jesus, and service to others. The focus
on defending the boundaries between righteous insiders and sinful outsiders is subordinate to relating to outsiders with compassion and dialogue. It is more open to learning new things from
God in prayer and from others. It is significantly less likely to
harbor racist attitudes.[8] Jesus calls for a new basis of community—
a basis in God's present, compassionate forgiveness, God's love
for the enemy, God's giving rain and sun to the just and unjust
alike.

There is also a third kind of Christianity: the mutually ignoring kind. This is an individualistic Christianity that says what
everyone does is his or her own business, and we have no right
to interfere in others' ethics. In this kind, we do not raise any
questions with our brothers or sisters about the speck in their
eye. But I do not think this is what Jesus advocates. He really is
saying that when we take the log out of our own eye, we can be
of more help to our fellow community members. Healthy community needs forgiveness for sure; it also needs mutual help.
Most of us have grown up not getting all the help we required
at some stage in our lives. We seek community where people
will forgive one another, and where they give one another help,
encouragement, and gentle suggestions.

BECOMING MUTUALLY FORGIVING FOLLOWERS OF JESUS

How can we become mutually forgiving followers of Jesus
rather than judgmental Christians? The teachings about not
judging are clear, but it is no small feat to practice the kind of

deep and abiding forgiveness that this part of the Sermon on the Mount asks of us. The late and much beloved teacher Lew Smedes wrote *Forgive and Forget,* which has helped thousands of people answer that question. So far it has sold half a million copies.

Lew was a man of wonderful compassion. Because he felt such compassion for so many, he filled his book with stories of people who had to travel from resentfulness to forgiveness for the health of their own selves. He was professor of Christian ethics at Fuller Theological Seminary in Pasadena, California. It is poetically symbolic, though tragic, that he died putting up Christmas lights, when his ladder suddenly fell. Christmas is the time when God truly becomes present to us sinners, when God enters our lives in Jesus. Lew was a follower of Jesus; he entered into the lives of others with compassion.

Recently a woman I have never met, who lives two thousand miles away, phoned me. She said she had been through a bitter divorce that left her with enormous resentment. She had finally found healing through reading Lew's two books, *Forgive and Forget* and *The Art of Forgiving.* She said she wanted to give him her profound thanks for the healing his books had brought to her, but she could not because he had just died. So she was calling me, his successor at Fuller, because she needed to thank *someone.* She was thanking *me* for the two books *Lew* had written, and for the healing they had brought to her life! It was the easiest gratitude I ever received. I was deeply grateful for the healing that had come to her life, and for the compassionate person Lew was. He showed compassion and support to me too, his fledgling successor.

Because the way he talks about forgiveness is so compelling, it's worth looking at his ideas in more depth.

The first step in developing forgiveness, Lew wrote, is to acknowledge that you were hurt unfairly, unjustly. Some hurts are minor and simply call for a sense of humor; if we work on forgiving them, it turns forgiving into something too light. The humor is the forgiveness. Other hurts are personal, unjust, and deep. They are likely to fester and cause us ongoing problems as well as complicate our relationships ("You did not deserve the hurt. It went deep enough to lodge itself in your memory. And it keeps on hurting you now").[9]

Unjust hurts may not have been intentional; a person can hurt us deeply even without thinking about it. To give the excuse that "I did not intend to hurt you" does not solve the problem or take away the hurt. The key is that it was wrongful, not deserved, unfair and unjust, and it brought great hurt.

The hurt is even worse if the other person seemingly broke the relationship casually, lightly, or thoughtlessly. You say, "I thought he cared about me deeply and would treat me with deep respect, but instead he broke the relationship without even paying attention to the hurt it caused—in spite of my having given myself faithfully to the commitment I thought we were growing with each other."

An unjust injury hurts you more deeply and with more jagged edges if it repeats the kind of hurt that set you back as a person in an earlier relationship. In fact, becoming aware that this present hurt repeats a previous personal drama can give you insight into the intensity of the hurt this time. It is not only what this present person has done to you; it tears at your selfhood where you still have scars from an early wound. Being aware of this can help understand why you feel so deeply hurt this time. It probably means you need to work on forgiveness toward both this person and the one who wounded you in the past as well.

Here is a key: recognizing that what needs forgiving is an *unjust* hurt makes it clear that the very act of forgiving is also an act of naming the wrong that occurred. Forgiving is by no means pretending the wrong did not occur. If I know I have done something to hurt another person wrongly, and if I work up the courage to apologize and the person says, "Oh, it doesn't matter; nothing to it," then I do not feel forgiven. If the other person says, "I don't even remember that you did that," then he or she can hardly extend forgiveness. But the person might say, "Yes, and it hurt a lot. And it has made me wonder if we could ever work together again. But I am willing to work together on defining some new ground rules." Then there is a possibility for forgiveness. Forgiveness includes realistic recognition that an injustice was done.

Knowing that forgiveness is a possibility can help us face the wrong realistically and truthfully rather than practicing denial and whitewashing it. Lew Smedes wrote: "There is no real forgiving unless there is first relentless exposure and honest judgment. When we forgive evil we do not excuse it, we do not tolerate it, we do not smother it. We look the evil full in the face, call it what it is, let its horror shock and stun and enrage us, and only then do we forgive it."[10]

Some people say that a particular evil was too evil, too monstrous, too irredeemably hurtful; they can never forgive it. They feel somehow that forgiving it would be doing a favor to the perpetrator. But according to Lew:

> [I]f we say that monsters are beyond forgiving, we give them a power they should never have. Monsters who are too evil to be forgiven get a stranglehold on their victims; they can sentence their victims to a lifetime of unhealed pain. If they are unforgivable monsters, they are given power to keep their evil alive in the hearts of those who suffered most. We give them power to condemn their victims to live forever with the hurting memory of their painful pasts. We give the monsters the last word.[11]

The worse the injustice and the more hurtful it was, the more the victim needs to be able to work slowly toward some kind of forgiveness to avoid living forever as a captive of bitterness, resentment, and hate. It is not fair to deny the victim the right to grow a modest garden of release and new life. It is most unfair to give that power to the worst of victimizers.

The second step in forgiveness is to begin overcoming hate and the lust for getting even. It helps if you admit to yourself that you really have hate and in fact wish for some kind of re-venge. I have observed good people, really good persons, who would never say they were seeking revenge but whose actions and words have an edge of spite. Sometimes it comes out as sar-casm, sometimes as a demand for special consideration or reduc-ing the amount of praise or privilege the other person has. Sometimes it comes out as a fantasy or daydream of wanting to do violence to someone. Many of us would never say that we hate someone else, but we might admit we have a major prob-lem with resentment. It has caused physical symptoms, a com-petitive drive, a passion to oppose injustice, and actions that we are not proud of but that we justify at the time because we have good grounds for resentment. (Maybe *resentment* is a polite term for hate used by a follower of Jesus who would say he or she is committed to love and not hate?) You affirm your passion to oppose injustice, but you do not want it to be based on seeking revenge, and you do want it to point to realistic, constructive ad-vocacy for transforming initiatives of change. But let's be clear: even though you are moving into forgiveness, Lew said, it does not mean you are not angry: "If you do not get angry and stay angry when a bad thing happens, you lose a piece of your humanity."[12]

Lew told of a budding friendship that he and his wife, Doris, were building with Doreen and Ted, when sudden mutual offense and anger closed off the relationship. Both sides felt un-justly hurt, and Doreen and Ted refused to talk about it, answer questions, or recognize that Lew and Doris existed. Mutual for-giveness was needed but seemed impossible, since no conversa-tion was forthcoming. Lew described what he and Doreen did:

> Doreen and I moved toward forgiveness *as we made three shifts in our feelings* about our falling-out.
>
> First, *we reduced our stakes.* In the early stage of our petty falling-out, we invested massive emotional resources in triv-ial offenses. We put our personal self-esteem on the block. We inflated the stakes beyond anything like their real worth. . . .

But [after] time . . . we let each other's faults melt down to their real size. And our pain melted with our anger as we scaled down our mutual indictments. . . .

Second, *we reduced what we expected from forgiveness.* . . . Once we understood that we did not *have* to be close friends after we forgave each other, that we did not *have* to come together the way we wanted it earlier, our worried resentments receded as a spring flood slips back into the soft earth. . . .

Third, *we reduced our desire for an even score.* We gave up trying to keep score of who did what to whom and how badly it hurt. We learned to leave the loose ends dangling, the scales off balance, to accept a score that neither of us could make come out even.[13]

The third step in developing forgiveness is finding some kind of empathy for the perpetrator, though not for the hurtful deed. For this, it helps to be aware that you have hurt others also—to become aware of the log in your own eye. It is knowing that you need forgiveness too.

This also helps reduce your desire for revenge. A major part of reducing desire for revenge is developing a realistic mental picture of the limitations, problems, or desires that the other person has in his or her life. Ordinary people as well as national leaders often make a major error when they think that an undeserved hurt was done for the intentional purpose of hurting us, when in fact it was done for some other reason.

Twenty-year-old Sue was dating Bill, but her mother thought the relationship was wrong. Her mother came to me, sobbing: "Why is Sue doing this to me?" I replied, "Maybe she doesn't think she is doing this to you; maybe she thinks she is doing something with Bill." My explanation was probably accurate, but I doubt it helped Sue's mother significantly. She was interpreting Sue's action as an action aimed against her.

Sometimes it helps to practice listening prayer, asking God for a vision of the problems and limitations that the other person is living with. The love Jesus teaches us is not sentimental affection for another but realistic understanding of the other's concerns. This is why he teaches us to "do unto others as you would have others do to you." And "love your neighbor as yourself." Jesus' love commands mean you try to envision imaginatively and realistically what problems your neighbor may be concerned about. They do not all revolve around an intention to do something to you. It often helps simply to ask the other person what he or she is concerned about. This can help in understanding the motivation for their action.

Lew Smedes wrote that his wife, Doris, "taught me a love that makes forgiving possible." He also gave thanks for "Christ's gift of forgiving love in my own life; I thank God for inventing the way to heal the hurts we don't deserve." He said we forgive others "by the alchemy of love": "Love is the power behind forgiveness. But it does not work the way a lot of people suppose. Love is not a soft and fuzzy sentiment that lets people get away with almost everything, no matter what they do to us." Jesus' kind of love confronts others when they need confronting. But the key is understanding the other.[14] Jesus' kind of love enters into the situation of the other, the way the Good Samaritan enters into the ditch where the Jew is lying, wounded. Jesus' kind of love gives more possibilities for understanding the other, and the other's limitations, realistically.

We always feel like an innocent lamb when someone hurts us unfairly. But we are never as pure as we feel. I may have been betrayed, cheated, maligned, and in other ways badly abused, and feel as if I am as benign as a shorn sheep. But being abused does not make me a good person. As Reinhold Niebuhr kept telling us years ago: "There is a labyrinth of motives in every heart; and every action, both good and evil, is the consequence of a complicated debate and tension within the soul." We are all too complex to be pure.[15]

The fourth step that completes the process of forgiveness is to reestablish the freedom and happiness of friendship—or at least welcome the other person back into a positive relationship. As the Apostle Paul says, "Welcome one another, therefore, just as Christ has welcomed you" (Rom. 15:7).

If the other person repeatedly causes physical abuse, or is a threat to your health, or imposes an unethical relationship, separation may be the best outcome. But there is a difference between separation grounded in resentment, hate, and malice, and separation that admits the reality of the limits and nevertheless wishes the other well.

One of the most common and difficult situations many people encounter is the need to forgive parents or other close friends or relatives for wrong and hurt. In many cases, the other person may not be well enough or open enough to face honestly the hurt that happened—or may even have died—so direct reconciliation is not possible. Sometimes it is possible to share the story with a third person, a friend, or a counselor who can take the place of the parent and offer an open confession of hurt and a wish for reconciliation to happen. I once had a falling out with a person who was too filled with resentment and alcoholism to allow himself to participate in reconciliation, despite many efforts. It was partly my fault. The lack of reconciliation weighed heavily on me for years. Then, serendipitously, I had dinner with a close friend of the person. After I told my story, he shared that the same falling out had happened between him and the other person as well. We empathized with each other's hurt. Together we experienced a kind of vicarious reconciliation in which we each could stand in for that person who was unwilling to reconcile. The heavy weight lifted.

To reestablish community and relationship, both parties must bring truthfulness and honesty about their real intentions. This includes honesty about the reality of the pain and responsibility for it. It does not mean agreement about every aspect; when people are involved in deep and complex hurts and healings their own heart is involved, and the heart shapes perception. It is almost guaranteed that some of the perceptions will differ. But honesty means, insofar as possible, being in touch with the reality of the hurt and responsibility for it. If the honesty can be shared, it is sometimes possible to have a deeper relationship than before, because you have shared together the enactment of hurt, honesty, and healing. This is a rare thing in life. At the same time, some defensiveness, guardedness, or distance, all of which are difficult ever to overcome, are likely to coexist along with the new depth of sharing in hurt and healing. We still have a speck in our eye, but we give thanks for the speck that has been removed, and for the beam of light that shines in.

9

Practicing Loyalty to God, Not to Worldly Powers

We have now arrived at the verse that is the most puzzling, mysterious, and indeed baffling of all in the Sermon on the Mount: "Do not give what is holy to dogs; and do not throw your pearls before swine; or they will trample them under foot and turn and maul you" (Matt. 7:6). Scholars agree that Jews of that time meant Gentiles (non-Jews) when they said "dogs" and "pigs." That is clear enough. But what in the world does Jesus mean by "holy things" and "pearls"? To figure out the answer, we need to determine the context of this verse. What other verses does it belong with?

Some try to interpret Matthew 7:6 as continuing the theme of the teaching against judging others that we discussed in the preceding chapter. To them, the verse contradicts those teachings because it seems to say that we *should* actually judge who are dogs and who are pigs and deny them what is holy and valuable. Has Jesus suddenly realized that his teaching about not judging is too radical and therefore is taking it back (at least partially), saying we *should* judge Gentiles, we *should* deny them what is holy? This does not seem right. Nowhere does Jesus ever decide he is too radical and contradict himself or take it back.

Others try to interpret it as a solitary verse, with no relationship to others in the Sermon on the Mount. In this view, maybe the holy things and the pearls mean the gospel. But this would mean we should not give the gospel to Gentiles. That would not make sense, though, because it contradicts the Great Commission in Matthew 28:19–20 ("Go therefore and make disciples of all nations, baptizing them in the name of the Father, and of the Son and of the Holy Spirit, and teaching them to obey everything that I have commanded you"). Nor is it consistent with Jesus' actions in healing the Gentile Canaanite woman's daughter later in Matthew. So what does Jesus mean in this enigmatic teaching?

LOYALTY TO GOD

The key is to realize that this verse belongs with the verses that follow it, Matthew 7:7–12. The pattern of threefold teachings that we have been seeing gives us this clue. Matthew 7:6 is the beginning verse of the last of the threefold teachings. Once we notice this, we can see its meaning by looking at the meaning of the verses that follow it, 7:7–12 (Figure 9.1). Then those other verses can give us clues about what is meant by holy things.

Traditional Righteousness: Do Not Give Holy Things to the Romans

This "mysterious verse" about holy things, dogs, pearls, and swine looks exactly like the other teachings of traditional righteousness that we have seen as a consistent pattern in the Sermon on the Mount. First, it resembles traditional Jewish teachings that call Gentiles dogs or pigs. Second, it begins with a negative "do not," as the other traditional teachings in Matthew 6:1–7:5 do. Third, it is followed by a description of a vicious cycle, and then the transforming initiatives about asking God for what we need, as you can see in Figure 9.1.

We find important clues about the meaning from those other verses as we further explore the rest of the teaching, but first let's note something specific about "dogs and pigs," which

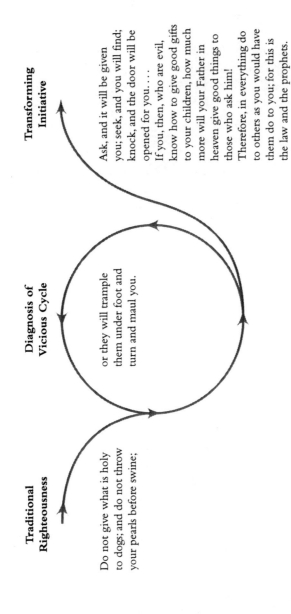

Traditional Righteousness

Do not give what is holy to dogs; and do not throw your pearls before swine;

Diagnosis of Vicious Cycle

or they will trample them under foot and turn and maul you.

Transforming Initiative

Ask, and it will be given you; seek, and you will find; knock, and the door will be opened for you....
If you, then, who are evil, know how to give good gifts to your children, how much more will your Father in heaven give good things to those who ask him!
Therefore, in everything do to others as you would have them do to you; for this is the law and the prophets.

Figure 9.1. Practicing Loyalty to God, Not to Economic and Political Powers.

clearly refer to Gentiles. What kind of Gentiles? The rabbis of Israel in their commentaries on scripture from the time just before Jesus and after Jesus always mean whole Gentile nations, not individual Gentiles. When they speak of "pigs," they usually mean Romans in particular, presumably because the Romans ate pork and regularly sacrificed a pig over a grave in order to sanctify it.

We can see it in the New Testament as well. When the Prodigal Son went into "the far country" and worked for "a citizen," where he got the job of feeding pigs, he was probably somewhere in the Roman Empire working for a Roman citizen, who ate pork. Similarly, in Mark 5:1–13, telling about the healing of the demon-possessed man in the Gerasene region (a Gentile region), Jesus asks the man's name. He answers: "My name is Legion." This is the word that means a Roman legion. The unclean spirits are sent into a herd of pigs, but pigs do not travel in herds. The Greek word for herd, however, was used for a band of Roman soldiers. Jesus "dismissed" the demons, which is the word for a military command. They rushed into the sea, which suggests troops rushing into battle. It could hardly be more obvious that the cursed pigs in this passage are being described as being like Roman troops. The pigs rush into the sea, as many Jews wished the Roman legion would do.[1] So when Jesus said "Do not throw your pearls before pigs," he was almost surely talking about Romans or the Roman Empire.

What does it mean to give the Romans your pearls and your holy things? To answer that, we need to see the rest of the teaching.

The Vicious Cycle: They Will Turn and Destroy You

The vicious cycle and its consequence follow: "They will trample them under foot and turn and tear you into pieces." Being "trampled under foot" is the fate that Jesus says salt deserves when it loses its distinctiveness by compromising with the world

(Matt. 5:13). I think that here too Jesus warns about compromise with the world, in this case with the Roman power structure that was so unjust and violent. Similarly, in Matthew 22:21, where the question is whether to pay loyalty to the Roman Empire in the form of giving or rendering taxes to the emperor, Jesus uses the same key Greek word as here in Matthew 7:6–12, *didomi* ("give" or "render"); "Do not *give* what is holy to dogs." There too, the climax of his teaching is to "Give to God the things that are God's." All three teachings are about giving full loyalty to God and God's way, and not giving our loyalty to the world and its powers.

Jesus often warned against the temptation of seeking prestige, honor, and wealth within the system of the powers and authorities in the world. He warned against neglecting the weightier matters of the Law of Moses—justice, faithfulness, and mercy—and neglecting to do anything to lift the burden of the needy (Matt. 23:4 and 23). His own temptation during his forty days in the wilderness was to seek to rule over the world by Satan's means, and he opposed it by teaching loyalty to God alone: "Worship the Lord your God, and serve only him" (Matt. 4:8–10).

That is again what Jesus teaches here in verses 6 through 12: worship the Lord your God, and serve only God, not the prestige and power of the Roman Empire. The danger and corruption of giving loyalty to the Roman Empire is also the temptation against which the Book of Revelation warns. The empire did indeed trample Jerusalem under foot and tear it to pieces in 70 A.D., and they did destroy the temple as Jesus predicted five times in the Gospels.

Transformation and Deliverance:
Give Your Trust to God

In the climax of the teaching, we are told to give *our trust, our loyalty,* and *our prayers* to our Father in Heaven, who will care for us as parents care for their children. God knows how to give good gifts; "dogs" and "pigs" do not. As in the previous teachings, the transforming initiative brings us into the presence of the dynamically present Father who graciously gives us good things. God is worthy of our trust and loyalty.

Giving loyalty and trust to the Roman Empire, in search of prestige, power, and wealth, was a temptation much present in the first century. Rome had the power to support or depose the Jewish ruling authorities in Jerusalem, and to grant or remove positions that could gain wealth. It had the power and wealth to reward those who served their injustices rather than be faithful to the God of Israel. The Jewish Sadducees and high priests had a reputation for taking this bait, compromising with Rome's corrupting influence and in that way acquiring their power and prestige illegitimately—which they then used to get more power and wealth. They had private police gangs that cooperated with the Romans to suppress any hint of rebellion. The high priests Annas and Caiaphas obtained their authoritarian power by collaborating with the Roman army's occupation of Israel. The priestly aristocracy lived in shocking luxury and extravagance while ordinary people grew poorer because of greedy policies.

U.S. readers know this temptation. The United States has more wealth and political, military, and corporate power than any nation in history—including Rome. We as its citizens are enormously tempted to worship such power. We are tempted to try to get ahead by giving support to powers that promise advancement and security even when those powers take advantage of their workers, damage the environment, or fail to contribute to the common good and the needs of their society. We have all seen, as this teaching says, that putting our trust in the powers that be can point to a future in which they "will turn and maul you." We can see this self-destructive future in national budget deficits and trade deficits growing out of control because of policies that reward the very powerful with wealth and take from the less powerful. We are depleting natural resources without regard to future generations. Much mass media entertainment seeks profits by spreading unethical values and showing immorality being rewarded, contrary to sexual faithfulness and the value and dignity of human life. The quality of public services such as schools, health care, hospitals, public transportation, levees, and bridges decays as the powerful shift money to serve their short-term interests. Nuclear, biological, and chemical weapons treaties are blocked because the powerful push an ideology of national selfishness rather than international inspection. These are facts that many do not want to face, but they are facts. As Jesus warned, the temple would be destroyed and people should flee to the hills when war came (Mark 13 and Matt. 24). Should not truthful assessment today warn that the temptation to get ahead by supporting temporal powers rather than the way of Jesus is having disastrous consequences?

The teaching is about the temptation to acquire special privileges by siding with the powerful and ignoring their injustice and violence. This is why it connects directly with Jesus' Prayer: "Lead us not into temptation."

It is a teaching about prayer as well. It warns us to give our prayerful concerns to God and not to political, economic, and ideological powers. Sometimes this passage is misinterpreted as promising that everyone who prays will get what he or she asks for. Most of us experience praying that does not always produce what we ask for: "For as the heavens are higher than the earth, so are my ways higher than your ways and my thoughts than your thoughts" (Isa. 55:9). We pray humbly, and we humble ourselves before God's ways, which are often beyond our understanding. Even Jesus prayed in Gethsemane that "this cup" would pass from him; he did not receive an affirmative answer. But God's ways are far more faithful than those of dogs and pigs, who are temporarily powerful. Their ways point toward destruction. This teaching means God is faithful and the Roman power structure is not. Put your trust and loyalty in God and God's ways, not in the temporary rewards of the dogs and pigs—the powers that promise us rewards.

THE GOLDEN RULE AND
THE SHAPE OF LOVE

The concluding verse (7:12) is part of the same theme. In the
Greek, the verse begins with "Therefore." The King James and
New International Version get this right, but many other translations fail to translate the "therefore." They just leave it out. It
should read, "*Therefore,* in everything do to others as you would
have them do to you." That is to say: therefore, as God gives you
good gifts, you give good deeds to others. Beginning the verse
with *therefore* connects it with the previous verses about God
giving good things. God's giving us good gifts is the reason and
the model for our doing good for others. Once again, Jesus'
teaching concludes a section by putting us in the presence of
our loving heavenly Father.

Furthermore, this concluding verse is the climax of the
whole central section, which begins with Matthew 5:17 ("I
have not come to abolish the law and the prophets") and ends
here at 7:12 with "For this is the law and the prophets." The two
verses match each other, referring to both the law and the
prophets. They are like bookends, framing the fourteen teachings of the Sermon on the Mount. Jesus says that the law and
the prophets are summarized by doing good to others as God
does good to us. This verse resembles the climax of 5:21–48
(Love your enemies as God gives sun and rain to the just and
unjust alike). In fact, throughout the Sermon on the Mount
God's merciful love shapes the kind of love we perform as followers of Jesus and as participants in the in-breaking of God's
reign: let God's love for the enemy shape the nature of our love
for our enemy. Let God's presence in secret call us to give our
loyalty to God in secret. Let God's reign and delivering justice
guide us as we make our financial investments. Let God's forgiveness and faithfulness guide us as we practice forgiving others
rather than judging them. Let God's trustworthiness guide us in

giving our loyalty to God rather than to the temporarily power-ful. Let God's giving us good gifts shape our love toward others. These teachings point to the source for a profound under-standing of love.

The first aspect of the kind of love Jesus teaches is that love is a way of discerning what others would want us to do for them because we can identify with their needs and interests just as we identify with our own needs and interests ("Do to others as you would have them do to you"). Love is not simply a romantic emotion or sentimental feeling. Love is grounded in God's love, forgiveness, and mercy. As God enters into our lives in Christ, love enters into the concerns of others and takes initiative toward others, even where there is hostility.

People who are beset by the personality disorder known as narcissism have a hard time entering into the concerns and per-spectives of another because they think it would require reject-ing their own concerns and perspectives. A narcissistic person cannot affirm his or her own perspective while also under-standing someone else's. If I am narcissistic, either I see things my way and reject all other ways as a threat to my perspective or else I affirm their perspective and deny my own. If you have ever been around narcissists you know the difficulty in dealing with them. They can seem quite irrational and oblivious until you understand that they see everything only through their own needs and desires. Jesus' love, by contrast, encourages a way of perception that encompasses others' as well as our own percep-tions. It can sense empathically what another person cares about without losing one's own sense of self. In fact, by being able to understand others one develops a richer and wiser self.

This is a lot like being multilingual. Because my sons lived a year in Germany and France and learned to speak another lan-guage, they can imagine how the news looks to many Euro-peans, in addition to how it looks to them as Americans. They can see things (partly) from more than one angle. This does not threaten their selfhood; it gives them a richer perspective. Having two eyes is better than having only one. Love of others that enters into how others feel enriches our understanding of the world.

The second aspect of the kind of love Jesus teaches is that it includes deeds of thoughtfulness for others. Love entails both entering into others' perspectives and doing something about it. So Jesus does not merely say, "Feel about others as you would have them feel about you." He says, *do* unto others. This is hardly an accident of one word in one verse. He emphasizes *doing* in the following verses as well: "Not everyone who says to me 'Lord, Lord,' will enter into the kingdom of heaven, but only the one who *does* the will of my Father in heaven"; "Everyone who hears these words and *does* them will be like a wise man. . . .'"; "Every good tree *produces* good fruits." All of these teachings use the same Greek word for *does,* including the one translated as "produces good fruits."

Jesus' most extensive teaching on the shape of love is the Parable of the Compassionate Samaritan (Luke 10:29–37). In the story, the Samaritan does nine deeds of deliverance. He goes to the wounded victim, pours wine on his wounds, pours oil on them, bandages them, puts him on the Samaritan's own animal, brings him to the inn, takes care of him, pays for further care, and promises to come back and pay any more that is needed. Parables are concise; by including so many deeds of deliverance Jesus tells us that deeds of deliverance are crucial to compassionate love.

The third aspect of Jesus' kind of love is that it involves confrontation of those who are not acting lovingly. Jesus' parable directly confronts priests who pass by the wounded Samaritan, as well as Jews who hate and exclude Samaritans. Love is not mere sentimentality; it includes the toughness of confronting those who exclude other human beings from community. Martin Luther King Jr.'s book *Strength to Love* describes profoundly and beautifully the shape of Christian love that Jesus teaches—all four of the dimensions that I name here. King led millions in seeing the realistic power of love to bring change where resistance to change was woven into the culture, habits, politics, laws, and power structures for generations. He embodied love of enemy and he spread it, teaching that we should consider the enemy to be injustice, not people. His kind of love explicitly included confrontation of injustice. He called it tough love with a tender heart.

Finally, the kind of love Jesus teaches seeks justice for others. Love knows that many people are hurt, excluded, dominated, and oppressed by injustice. In his book *Why We Can't Wait,* King wrote movingly about the customs and policies that block the growth and the future of many children in the world. He called all of us to love in a way that does deeds correcting the injustice that keeps children from fully maturing into the people God intended them to be. The Parable of the Compassionate Samaritan directly calls us to oppose the injustice that excludes other racial groups from respectable society and human fulfillment.

REPENT: CHANGE YOUR LOYALTIES AND YOUR ACTIONS

Jim Wallis, editor of *Sojourners* magazine, has written a wonderful book on repentance, *The Call to Conversion.*[2] He defines *repentance* as facing up honestly to our past (including misplacing our loyalty in the powers that be) and turning from it to God. As he says, "The Old Testament word for conversion (*shub*) means 'to turn, return, bring back, restore.' It occurs more than one thousand times and always involves turning from evil and to the Lord." It is the key to conversion.

> Turning around involves stopping and proceeding in a new direction. The New Testament stresses the necessity of a radical turnabout and invites us to pursue an entirely different course of life. Thus, fundamental change of direction is central to the meaning of the words. . . . The Bible refers to our self-determined course as walking in sin, darkness, blindness, dullness, sleep, and hardness of heart. To convert is to make an

about-face and take a new path. . . . Thus conversion is far more than an emotional release and much more than an intellectual adherence to correct doctrine. It is a basic change in life direction.[3]

Conversion requires that we participate in the reign of God with our whole self, not merely internal attitudes. When we repent, we redirect our loyalty in our particular historical situation. It never happens in a historical vacuum: "We are converted to compassion, justice, and peace as we take our stand as citizens of Christ's new order." Repentance happens "in the midst of concrete historical events, dilemmas, and choices."[4]

One of the seven characteristics of the reign of God that we noticed in Chapter Two is a return to God. Jesus says, as Isaiah did, that we are exiled from God, giving our loyalties to other power centers—money, prestige, advancement, political power, what Wallis calls the "reigning idolatries." Repentance involves returning to serving God with full integrity, with our whole self. It is a return to loving our enemies as God does, and to peacemaking and faithfulness among people, including faithfulness in telling the truth. It is a return to worshiping God and serving God for the sake of our loyalty to God, not in order to be seen by others. It is a return to investing our money in God's causes. It is a return to practicing mutual forgiveness rather than being judgmental. Repentance is about feeling sorry and about turning and returning to God with our whole self.

Conversion is not just for non-Christians by any means. It is a continual process for followers of Jesus. The Holy Spirit is always surprising us, calling us to new changes. We see this again and again in the Book of Acts, as the Holy Spirit keeps calling Jewish followers of Jesus to repent and accept Samaritans, Gentiles, an Ethiopian eunuch, and even the Roman prison guards as fellow followers of Jesus and members of Christian churches. The Holy Spirit calls Jesus' followers to share their wealth with the poor and the needy. Conversion is about engaging in some new practices of evangelism, of welcoming community, and of sharing, and also about the joy of the Holy Spirit breaking into our lives and creating a new drive to follow Jesus in a way that does not pay attention to the need to conform to the powers and authorities. The life of a follower of Jesus is a life of learning new dimensions of discipleship every day. We follow a way of continual repentance, continual transformation and growth. Jim Wallis writes:

> The kingdom indeed represents a radical reversal for us. Aggrandizement, ambition, and aggression are normal to us and to our society. Money is the measure of respect, and power is the way to success. Competition is the character of most of our relationships, and violence is regularly sanctioned by our culture as the final means to solve our deepest conflicts. . . . To convert means to commit our lives unreservedly to Jesus Christ, to join his new order, and to enter into the fellowship of the new community. Our sins are forgiven, we are reconciled to God and to our neighbor, and our destiny becomes inextricably bound to the purposes of Christ in the world.[5]

In the early church, because Christians lived distinctly different from their surrounding culture, they had to be ready to explain themselves. This is no longer true. Christians now live so much like everyone else that the proclamation of the gospel is severely damaged. Jesus' name is probably more frequently mentioned in public now than at any time in U.S. history, yet the content of his teaching is shockingly ignored. Christians serve money, power, and success about as much as others do.

In the matter of nuclear weapons, for example, our moral sensitivities are numbed. We have responsibility for a nuclear arsenal that some day may destroy almost everyone living, yet few of us gather together to demand mutual force reduction. We have put trust not only in the leaders but in the missiles themselves. Most former government officials of both parties who previously had responsibility for these weapons recommend treaty agreements for mutual reduction by steady steps to a smaller and smaller number. Yet it does not happen. Is this not a call for the kind of repentance that Jesus talks about, and for the kind of shift of trust to God that he calls for? Only the presence of Jesus Christ in our hearts, working our own conversion, can turn us to being faithful, and in that way to become safer.

In much the same way, the Bible is full of teachings on justice for the poor. Justice for the poor is the second most frequent teaching in the Old Testament (after idolatry). One of every ten verses in the Gospels of Matthew, Mark, and Luke is about relations between rich and poor. Yet many prominent Christians, including many evangelicals today (Wallis identifies as an evangelical), have mostly not called for economic justice for the poor. Instead they have supported the interests of the powers that be through tax breaks for wealthy people and corporations. What is wrong? Have we given our loyalty to the powers whose wealth and power and status we would like to have?

We are deeply engaged in a struggle—not with flesh and blood, but with the ruling powers and authorities, which includes the ideologies that give authority to power. Therefore we need the helmet of salvation, the breastplate of righteousness, the sword of the Spirit, and the shoes of peace (Eph. 6: 12–17). And we need prayer. Prayer recognizes that God is LORD, not the powers of Rome or the powers of our time. Prayer gives our loyalty to God, not to an ideology clinging to those suicidal nuclear weapons. It starts in confession and repentance and declares that our trust is in God, not a political ideology. Therefore prayer is central for the conversion that we need, especially prayer for our enemies whom we must begin to see as more like us than unlike us; they too have families, children, fears, and pressures.

Furthermore, it is not enough to just say no. Repentance and conversion turn away from false loyalty to the powers that be; they also turn toward loyalty to God, whose way is shown to us in Jesus. We need to follow the positive alternatives that Jesus gives to us, the practices that make for peace. These are the practices of the ethic of just peacemaking addressed in Chapter Five.

If we truly care, we will create churches and communities that invite the needy in with a new community whose life together is the beginning of God's new order (as we saw in Chapter Seven). We need a community of support that helps us strengthen our sense of mission as followers of Jesus such that we are truly different from the world. We will not do an effective job of resisting captivity of the church to ideologies of nationalism and domination by the powerful if we reduce "church" to only one hour a week of worship. We need community support, mutual forgiveness, and correction in a community of disciples who truly want to follow Jesus.

Kern Road Mennonite Church in South Bend, Indiana, for example, has timed Sunday worship service to be held immediately prior to the Sunday school classes. Then most people stay for the community support and discussion that comes in group classes. All Saints Episcopal Church in Pasadena has an early worship service, followed by Sunday school classes and then an 11:15 A.M. worship service. In both churches, people who come for worship are all encouraged to join a Sunday school class in which they study together what it means to follow Jesus in this complex world. This gives a much greater sense of community than coming for only a one-hour worship service. At Kern Road, all church members are assigned to a "shepherd's group" in the part of town where they live which meets once a month for discussion and fellowship.

In both churches, many of the members also belong to a small group with a mission. All Saints has more than fifty such groups. Many churches have small groups, but the key is they are *groups with a mission*. Their members have answered a call to work on a specific shared mission. Some groups support the Bread for the World program to combat world hunger (www.bread.org); others help families with a mentally retarded or mentally ill member; or run a mentoring program for children and teenagers in school; another may have an inward and outward journey of peacemaking as described in Every Church a Peace Church (www.ecapc.org); others may work on planting new churches; or support international missions of the church; or minister to the poor by volunteering in a community center or a hunger-feeding program; or work on living simply themselves and on supporting Creation Care (www.creationcare. org). And so on—there is no shortage of action needed in the world. If most members are engaged in small groups with a mission, power ideologies contradicting the way of Jesus Christ are less likely to manipulate and seduce a church.

REPENT FROM GIVING OUR LOYALTIES TO SECULAR POWERS

Jim Wallis's highly popular book *God's Politics: Why the Right Gets It Wrong and the Left Doesn't Get It,* says: "Abraham Lincoln had it right. Our task should not be to invoke religion and the name of God by claiming God's blessing and endorsement for all our national policies and practices—saying, in effect, that God is on our side. Rather, Lincoln said, we should pray and worry earnestly whether we are on God's side."[6]

Similarly, Martin Luther King Jr. combined references to the prophets of Israel, love of Jesus, and the patient work of God for justice with references to the Declaration of Independence, the Constitution, and the Bill of Rights in a way that included people rather than excluding them. He clearly identified the enemy as injustice, not particular people who resisted the efforts of the civil rights movement. He taught a whole movement to practice love of enemy. He taught us to sing "Black and White Together," and to work together for a beloved community that can all walk together toward the Promised Land. He never used God's name to endorse one race over another or one nation's war on another. He certainly did not use the name of Jesus to endorse policies that shift the wealth of the nation from the poor and working class to the wealthy and powerful corporations. It was when he went to Memphis to support justice for garbage workers that he was tragically shot dead.

Wallis is concerned that a dangerous theology of empire is emerging in America. He is concerned that "many people around the world now think Christian faith stands for political commitments that are almost the opposite of its true meaning. How did the faith of Jesus come to be known as pro-rich, pro-war, and only pro-American?"[7]

This, Wallis says, is what the right gets wrong. What the left does not get is the need for the language of faith. The left is too much influenced by Enlightenment rationalism and modern secularism, and so it is nervous about ever speaking of faith or God in public. Liberalism has lost evangelism.

Over and against this thin and sterile avoidance of faith language in public, many like Wallis are saying that the modern Enlightenment move to eliminate references to specific religious figures and instead trying to speak a universal moral *Esperanto*—a language with no references to faith or God—has failed, because:

1. We have new awareness that no language is universal; we are all influenced by our particular historical, cultural, and faith contexts, whether we admit it or not.

2. Pretending that we speak a universal language systematically blinds us to our own hidden loyalties, influences, and interests.

3. It produces a thin ethic lacking in the powerful motivation that many of us get from Jesus, the Qu'ran, or the Torah. We need to be able to speak our thick, rich faith languages and not to give them over to those who manipulate the language to eliminate its moral appeal and make it serve the interests of political and economic powers.

4. We are now discovering the joy of dialoguing respectfully among Muslims, Jews, Christians, Buddhists, and so on, not only about thin abstract principles but about the very beliefs that are important to them and us. The dialogue becomes much more interesting if each of us is allowed to say what matters to

us. We do not forbid specifics but instead learn respectfully from them about their tradition. This leads to more openness when we share our own faith and the way of Jesus. Interfaith dialogue and evangelism both become possible.

5. But the Enlightenment was right that religious language is sometimes misused to inflame a warring spirit. Therefore many of us seek to take Jesus back, highlighting how much Jesus teaches about peacemaking. We do not want the name of Jesus or God to endorse war. We also ask people of whatever faith, or no particular faith, to strengthen a shared cultural understanding: that use of religious language to endorse war and claim to be righteous while others are sinful, as the Pharisee did in Jesus' parable, is itself evil and dangerous.

6. So we need both the languages of particular faiths and also the shared cultural language of just peacemaking that is critical of the false prophets who use religious language to support policies of war and greed.

7. We need to be bilingual—to acknowledge the particular language that is dearest to our own faith community, and also to speak as much of a shared language as we can, such as human rights, what works to make peace, diagnoses of the evils of empire, naming the evils of terrorism and suicide bombing, and so forth.

In sum, we need a "thicker Jesus" than the thin rationalism of merely secular language. We need to let the true Jesus of the New Testament speak—fully, concretely, and specifically. We do not need a thin, silenced Jesus but a Jesus who speaks concretely and teaches as he does in the Sermon on the Mount.

How to Tell a True Ethic
from a False One

Living the teachings of the Sermon on the Mount, a way
that delivers us from our addictions rather than staying in
the throes of vicious cycles, is not only practical but
easier. In a deep sense, it is easier to live the way of deliverance
than the way of the vicious cycle. It is more rewarding to make
peace with others, embody faithfulness and truthfulness, pray
sincerely, and control our expenditures wisely than to try living
without those teachings, where we are driven by continuing and
unresolved hostility and deceit and judgment, pursuit of self-
aggrandizement, and loyalty to unjust powers. Living the Sermon
on the Mount is the way of grace. It is the way of Jesus. It is the
way of the breakthrough of the reign of God.

It might be my early background, when I thought I was going to be a physicist, but I am fascinated by the numerical cor-
respondences of these teachings we have been discussing. So
were people in the Jewish culture of Matthew's time. For example, the number seven occurs throughout the Bible, from the
seven days of creation in the Book of Genesis to the seven
churches, seven seals, seven plagues, and seven trumpets of the
Book of Revelation. It is therefore no accident that the large,
central section of the Sermon on the Mount that we have been
studying has fourteen threefold teachings. This neatly matches
the beginning of the Gospel of Matthew, which has three times

fourteen generations from Abraham to Jesus. To Matthew, in his Jewish culture, seven is a number of completeness and goodness, like the seven days in which God created the earth. Fourteen is double completeness and goodness. Three is also a number of completeness. So three times fourteen is triply doubly complete. It is good, really good.

Now we have finished the main section of the Sermon on the Mount, and we have arrived at the concluding section, Matthew 7:13–29, which also has three teachings. But now, in the conclusion, each one no longer has the triadic form of traditional teaching, vicious cycle, and transforming initiative. Here the teaching is a warning against being misled by false prophets into doing evil. Thus it connects with the final petition of Jesus' Prayer: "Deliver us from evil."

The question is, How do we tell which are the false prophets? How do we tell a true ethic from a false one? We all have an ethic: it is our way of life, our guiding pattern of how to be faithful people who contribute to the good of the community and the creation in which we live. Sometimes we can say clearly what pattern of practices, rules, principles, and virtues guides us in what we do, and other times we simply do it without talking about it. How can we tell a true guiding pattern from a false one? This question is all the more important in a time of encounter among religions and diverse cultures, as well as many temptations for Christian faith itself to go astray. Jesus gives us an answer that helps us know what is true without having to claim that we possess universal rational knowledge.

VICIOUS CYCLES OR JOYOUS ENTRY?

"Enter through the narrow gate; for wide is the gate and broad is the road that leads to destruction, and many enter through it. But small is the gate and narrow the road that leads to life, and only a few find it" (Matt. 7:13–14 NIV).

In this teaching, Jesus puts two contrasts before us. He speaks of the broad way and the narrow way. The broad way that many are taking is the way of vicious cycles. The narrow way is joyous participation in the reign of God. We need to choose; we cannot go two ways at once. The way to life is narrow because doing something right requires actually doing it the right way—which Jesus teaches us. There is just one way to do it right, and that is Jesus' way. Choose: Do you want the way of the vicious cycles, leading to destruction, or the way of the transforming initiatives, leading to life?

Jesus warns us here against missing the reign of God by failing to choose to follow his teachings. This warning is the parallel side of the joy of the beatitudes with which the Sermon begins. The beatitudes announce the joy of participating in God's reign. The warnings here name the judgment that comes from not doing Jesus' teachings and therefore missing out on God's reign. In the beatitudes we saw, in effect, "Joyous are you because you get to participate in the coming of God's reign." Here we see "Be warned; you might miss it if you choose the wrong way."

This choice between the two ways is like a long biblical tradition that reaches back to Deuteronomy 11:26–28: "I am setting before you today a blessing and a curse: the blessing, if you obey the commandments of the LORD your God that I am commanding you today; and the curse, if you do not obey the commandments of the LORD your God, but turn from the way that I am commanding you today, to follow other gods that you have not known." There are two ways; choose the way of the beatitudes, the way of joy, the way that leads to life.

If you carefully examine what Jesus says, you will find it surprising that so many well-meaning people—even the Revised Standard Version (and its cousin, the New Revised Standard Version)—speak not of broad and narrow but of the "easy" way and the "hard" way. Those two words appear nowhere in what Jesus taught here. The Greek word in "broad is the road" means broad, spacious, roomy. The Greek word in "narrow is the road" means compressed, narrowed, restricted. It does not mean hard. The New International Version, the New English Bible, and the King James Version translate it correctly. Personally, I do not know why this is, but it may be that when a presupposition about a teaching leads even a team of biblical translators to mistranslate not one word but two, and to repeat the error systematically in the new version of the translation, it is time to correct the error. Let us deliver Jesus' way from that off-putting preconception that it is hard and idealistic! Jesus' way is the way of deliverance from destruction, whereas remaining stuck in the way of the vicious cycles is a truly hard life. To live Jesus' way is in tune with how we were created—for fellowship, for faithfulness, for peace.

Sometimes I hear people who are invited to jump off a diving board, or study math, or learn a language, say, "Oh, that's hard" or "That's too hard." Maybe they mean to express respect for those who can do it. But they often mean they are afraid to try it. When people say, "Jesus' way is hard teachings," I do not know what to think. Maybe they intend to praise Jesus. Maybe they rightly say that it includes some self-sacrifice. Jesus had to die on a cross. If we really follow Jesus, we might be persecuted. In fact, it is right to question understandings of discipleship that require that we do only what is comfortable and never make any sacrifices. Almost every successful marriage requires significant sacrifice on the part of each partner, adapting to the ways, demands, and limits of the other. Every successful athlete knows it takes major sacrifice and some serious discipline to achieve success, but those efforts are much more worthwhile than choosing the lazy or mediocre way.

Still, sometimes it sounds as if people intend to praise Jesus' way while staying distant from venturing to do what Jesus calls them to do. When someone tells a school pupil again and again that learning math or English grammar is hard, I fear the pupil may become discouraged from believing she or he can ever learn it. Many young learners become blocked that way and never learn the subject the rest of their lives.

Jesus does not offer the option of praising his teachings as hard and then excusing yourself from doing them. Either you follow him or you do not. There is no third choice. Jesus asks us to choose life or destruction.

In Matthew 11:28–30, Jesus says, "Come to me, all you that are weary and are carrying heavy burdens, and I will give you rest. Take my yoke upon you, and learn from me, for I am gentle and humble in heart, and you will find rest for your souls. For my yoke is easy, and my burden is light."

I do not think Jesus' point is that his way is hard. Rather, his way is narrow in the sense of being definite: live specifically by these words and you will have life. In fact, many of us have found that living a life of hostility, bitterness, and resentment toward others, or a life of deceit and not telling the truth, or a life of worrying all the time about prestige and what others think of us, or a life of always wanting more money for ourselves, or condemning others and trying to please the powers that rule, is much harder than just living the way of Jesus. Perhaps we have learned the wise teaching of our elders: "If it's worth doing, it's worth doing right." Maybe we should add another teaching: "Doing things wrong causes nothing but problems." Or: "Doing things wrong makes life a mess."

Someone has said it well, that each way is like entering a funnel. You can enter at the wide end, but then the farther you go the more life closes down. It ends in destruction. Or you can enter a funnel at the narrow end, and the farther you go, the more it opens up into the joy of the reign of God. It ends in life.

FALSE PROPHETS

Beware of false prophets, who come to you in sheep's clothing but inwardly are ravenous wolves. You will know them by their fruits. Are grapes gathered from thorns, or figs from thistles? In the same way, every good tree bears good fruit, but the bad tree bears bad fruit. A good tree cannot bear bad fruit, nor can a bad tree bear good fruit. Every tree that does not bear good fruit is cut down and thrown into the fire. Thus you will know them by their fruits.

Not everyone who says to me, "Lord, Lord," will enter the kingdom of heaven, but only the one who does the will of my Father in heaven. On that day many will say to me, "Lord, Lord, did we not prophesy in your name, and cast out demons in your name, and do many deeds of power in your name?" Then I will declare to them, "I never knew you; go away from me, you evil-doers" [Matt. 7:15–23].

This is a warning. There will be false prophets. They will try to lead us astray. But who are the false prophets? How do we tell?

We do not know what specific group this passage in Matthew refers to. The leading possibility among scholars is that he is referring to Christians who were influenced by Greek or Hellenistic culture and were lax about doing the teachings of Jesus. Regardless of who Matthew meant, the point is that false prophets try to teach us something different from Jesus' way, and the result of their teaching is bad outcomes, bad fruits. We are therefore warned to watch out for leaders who claim to be Christians but who teach us to do something different from what Jesus calls us to do.

In the Gospel of Matthew, the only people who call Jesus Lord are his disciples and outsiders who sincerely come to him with a need for mercy and deliverance and who commit themselves to him. In this passage, false prophets are those who clearly claim to be Christians. They also ask, "Did we not prophesy in your name, and cast out demons in your name, and do many deeds of power in your name?" What's wrong with this? Nothing, really. Jesus favors such action in Matthew 10:7–8, but they do this to get recognition for themselves rather than meet people's needs. It is the opposite of those in Matthew 25 who meet people's needs and do not realize they are doing it for Jesus.

Matthew also warns about false prophets in other passages (24:4–5, 10–12, 23–28). Jesus says, "Then many will fall away, and they will betray one another and hate one another. And many false prophets will arise and lead many astray. . . . For false Messiahs and false prophets will appear and produce great signs and omens, to lead astray, if possible, even the elect" (Matt. 24:9–11, 24). In Jesus' time, false messiahs did organize rebellions against Rome, and they and their followers were killed by the Romans. Jesus warned against following them; it would lead to destruction of the temple. Instead, he said, when war came his followers should flee to the hills. They—we—were called to peacemaking, not to hate and participate in rebellion.

The Book of Revelation also describes "a false prophet" that speaks like a dragon but has the horns of a lamb. We are not sure what this means. The Book of Revelation has several cases of servants to the power of the Roman Empire who imitate the followers of the Lamb, Jesus, in some way. Having horns like a lamb may mean that it pretends to be a follower of Jesus. In other words, it dresses up to look like a lamb, a Christian, a pretend follower of Jesus, and tells us to give our loyalty to the ruler, even making a worship image of the ruler. "It deceives the inhabitants of the earth, telling them to make an image" for the ruling power (Rev. 13:1–18).

All these teachings mean that we should beware of those who claim to be Christian spokespersons but whose words tell us to give our loyalty to the ruling powers. They deceive us. We are to beware of those who claim to speak truth but whose words try to persuade us to serve greed, war, and ethnic division. Beware of those who put before us a corporate brand, or a national flag, or a racial loyalty, or the almighty dollar, or an image of our nation that stands for goodness against another nation that stands for evil and inflames us to make war and arouses our passions to serve that image rather than serve God who is revealed in Jesus Christ and in the Holy Spirit.

This pretend-lamb power lets "no one buy or sell who does not have the mark." I guess in our time the mark is the almighty dollar. If we are truthful with ourselves, we admit that much of our life is spent in service of the mark of the beast, the almighty dollar.

The Book of Revelation tells us that this pretend lamb has a mark on its forehead, the number 666. Some have said that the number value of the letters in the name of Nero Caesar add up to 666, and others have suggested other names. In any case, it is clear that biblically the number seven means perfection or goodness, and the number six means not-seven, or not-good. Whoever this pretend lamb is, the salient point is that it dresses up like a Christian and is not good. The text makes clear that this beast is headed for destruction.

In the Book of Revelation, the followers of the Beasts do violence, but the followers of the Lamb do not. Instead, they do the deeds that Jesus taught. Fourteen times (there's that number, fourteen, again!), the Book of Revelation says we can tell who the followers of the Lamb are because they do the deeds that Jesus taught (Rev. 2:2, 19, 23, 26; 3:8, 10; 9:20–21; 12:17; 14:4, 12; 16:11; 19:10; 20:12–13; 22:11). Each time the words differ somewhat—they do the will of God revealed in Jesus, the deeds that Jesus taught, the deeds that are God's will, and so on. Each time the point is the same, which is the point of the Book of Revelation, despite many strange interpretations: it may seem that the Beasts are in charge, but God really is Lord. The Beasts will lose and God will win. Trust in the way of God as revealed in Jesus. Follow the deeds that Jesus taught. The followers of the Lamb will be delivered from the destruction.

Since Jesus' teaching in Matthew 7:13–27 is a warning about false prophets, and warning to do things right by doing his teachings, it is clearly a warning about the danger of evil. Therefore it fits well with the final petition of the Lord's Prayer: "Deliver us from evil." The teachings of Jesus, we have seen repeatedly, warn us about the vicious cycles that alienate us from the reign of God. Jesus' teachings point the way of deliverance, as we have seen a number of times. I insist on this point because of the misperception that many of Jesus' teachings are impossible to follow—worthy, but hard and high ideals. Once again we have confirmation that the teachings of Jesus are to be interpreted as the way of deliverance. In being delivered by God from evil, we are given the empowering grace of the Holy Spirit to follow the way of Jesus, the way of deliverance from the vicious cycles.

BY THEIR FRUITS

We live in a time of growing awareness that there are many kinds of ethics. We encounter various religions and cultures. Many Christians are influenced by ideologies put forth by economic and political powers, by spokespersons on television who claim to be speaking for Christ but in fact seem to be urging us to support powerful political and economic rulers. Jesus' teachings here seem utterly pertinent to our time.

How do we tell who is a false prophet and which ethic is true?

Jesus gives us two clear clues. The first is to measure them by whether they urge us to do the deeds that Jesus teaches, or some other ideology. To make that measure, we require the thicker and deeper understanding of Jesus' way that is given to us in the Sermon on the Mount. Jesus says that the true prophets urge you to do what he has taught you. False prophets urge you to give your loyalty to some other ideology.

The second is to measure an ethic by its fruits. Recently a participant in a Sunday school class protested, "Since we all have our own beliefs and our own reasons for doing what we do, no one can say what's ethical and what isn't. We just have to agree to disagree." Anyone who believes in a genuinely Christian way of life should take this challenge seriously; in our current climate of moral relativism, can we talk about Christian ethics at all? The traditional moral strategy of the eighteenth century Enlightenment—building ethical arguments on indisputable truth claims, such as seeking the greatest good of the greatest number, or never treating others as only a means to one's own ends—has fallen on hard times. Consensus as to exactly which truth claims are indisputable has steadily diminished over time. Moreover, the world has seen enough racism, violence, and abuse perpetrated by those who claim to represent the truth to make us all wary of dogmatism and certainty. With fewer and fewer people persuaded by abstract moral arguments based on claims of universal truth, is it possible to validate an ethic, to say that this set of practices is Christian and this other is not?

When Jesus said, "By their fruits you shall know them," he authorized his followers to examine the long-term impact of guiding patterns and ethics and to judge their merit accordingly. This affirms that living in cooperation with God's Spirit will contribute tangibly to the kind of peace, justice, reconciliation, and human community characteristic of the Reign of God. In the words of H. Richard Niebuhr, "History is the laboratory in which our faith is tested." If there is such a thing as a true way of life, then we ought to be able to identify people and communities that followed this way in a manner that brought about faithful change in their world.[1]

Dietrich Bonhoeffer, of whom we have spoken many times in this book, is such a person. He translated the Way of Jesus, as described in the Sermon on the Mount, into a life of costly obedience, solidarity with the persecuted, and resistance to social evil at a time when the greater number of German Christians enthusiastically endorsed Hitler's agenda. Although in the minority, Bonhoeffer was not alone. Other Christian leaders, among them the French pastor André Trocmé, found in Jesus' teachings and practices resources for mobilizing an entire segment of the population against the seemingly unstoppable Nazi machinery. Together, Bonhoeffer and Trocmé incarnate the ethics of the way of Jesus and a model for discipleship that demonstrates the validity of Jesus' ethical teachings by the fruits they bear amid concrete social struggle.

After Bonhoeffer's death, Karl Barth, the leader of Christians who opposed Hitler's murderous policies, wrote that it was

Bonhoeffer who, most early and clearly, though at danger to his own life, stood up and spoke out in defense of Jews in Germany. Bonhoeffer saw that the church's nationalism and anti-Semitism contradicted its gospel and spelled disaster for society.

Bonhoeffer did not arrive at his position easily. Years earlier, at the University of Berlin, he absorbed the German liberal tradition and took for granted the social determinism that would later pave the way for Hitler's rise to power. But in 1930–31, while doing his postdoctoral study in New York and engaging deeply in the life of an African American Baptist church in Harlem, he discovered a more concrete way of discipleship centered on Jesus, and especially on the Sermon on the Mount. He made verse-by-verse explication of the Sermon on the Mount the focus of his classic work *The Cost of Discipleship*. Bonhoeffer's resistance to the Nazi regime and his solidarity with the Jews cannot be understood apart from his devotion to this particular biblical text. He began to perceive the evils of National Socialism, understand the shape that his resistance must take, and come alongside the persecuted Jews at the very time that his thinking and writing were being shaped by direct engagement with the Sermon on the Mount.

Across the continent, and unbeknownst to Bonhoeffer, the pastor of a small congregation in a remote French village was also following the Sermon on the Mount. Pastor André Trocmé and his wife, Magda, came to lead the Reformed church in the Huguenot town of Le Chambon in 1934. Trocmé's teaching and preaching emphasized the Sermon on the Mount and following Jesus, as Bonhoeffer did. After France fell to Germany in 1940, an escapee from a nearby concentration camp appeared at the Trocmés' door asking for help, and Magda invited her in. More followed, and the church members, shaped by Jesus-centered preaching, memories of persecution, and long habits of hospitality and generosity, followed the Trocmés' leadership in opening their homes. Over the next three years, the Chambonnais provided Jewish refugees with food and shelter, false IDs and ration cards, and in some cases transport to Switzerland. Increasing pressure from the Nazis led to the arrests of Trocmé and his colleague Roger Theis, and execution of his cousin Daniel Trocmé, but the work continued. By the time of France's liberation in 1944, citizens of the village had rescued between three and five thousand Jews from death—as many Jews as there were non-Jewish citizens of Le Chambon.

Like Bonhoeffer, Trocmé believed that the Sermon on the Mount was to be lived out concretely amid contemporary social struggle. He contended that Jesus rejected the two options of violent resistance to Roman oppression or passive withdrawal from political concerns, and that Jesus pioneered a new strategy of nonviolent struggle for human dignity and social justice. The church was to present a new social possibility to the world, to demonstrate that God's love for his enemies spoke more truthfully to the human situation than the politics of violence, and to suffer, even unto death, as a sign of patient confidence in God's ultimate victory.

I call Bonhoeffer and Trocmé's ethics Trinitarian and incarnational: Trinitarian because it attends to how God is revealed as Father, Son, and Spirit; incarnational because it understands Jesus not only as a doctrine but as the way of God specifically embodied in Jesus the human being, and because it enters bodily into real human struggles and human need. For Bonhoeffer and Trocmé, the Trinity was not a doctrinal curiosity to dissect and analyze but a concrete way to know God and to participate in his justice-making grace.

To know God as Father is to affirm that *God is sovereign over all of life*—that every aspect of life, not only the personal or religious—belongs under the scrutiny of Jesus' teachings. Both Bonhoeffer and Trocmé refused to compartmentalize life into a private realm under Christ's Lordship and a societal realm governed by supposed political or economic necessities. If we draw too sharp a line between God's kingdom and present history, between inner experience of faith and outer deeds of compassion, or between a personal relationship with God and a public commitment to God's justice, we invariably push Jesus and his teachings into a box, away from the real concerns of our daily lives. But if we recognize God as sovereign over all of life, we rediscover the social, economic, and political relevance of the ethics of the Gospels.

A moment's thought tells us why those Christians who clearly said God is sovereign over all of life have tested out much better in the laboratory of history. They did not fool themselves into thinking they were following God's will while limiting it to only one compartment of life and following some ideology of greed or hate or racism in the rest of life. Bonhoeffer, Trocmé, and their followers knew they were called to follow God's will in all of their relationships.

To know God as Son is to affirm that *in Jesus Christ, God has revealed God's will for human interaction.* Much of the work done in Christian ethics in the twentieth century avoided extensive reference to Jesus' teachings. It frequently defined Christian living in abstract terms such as love or forgiveness, not on the basis of careful biblical exegesis but according to the dominant secular theories of the day. By contrast, when we look for God's will revealed in Jesus, we find a specific social vision drawn from the Old Testament prophets and embedded in concrete practices: delivering the poor from poverty, opposing those who oppress the weak, ending violence, and welcoming outcasts into community. If the God of all creation is revealed in Jesus, then the Sermon on the Mount has something to say about how we perceive and respond to our world.

By contrast, some split the world into inner attitude and outer action, or being and doing, which Jesus never does, and then they limit Jesus' teachings to the inner self as if he says nothing about action, about doing, about practicing what he teaches. This is self-deception, convincing myself inside that I am a follower of Jesus while my actions show that I am following some economic or political ideology.

Jesus says, "You will know them by their fruits. . . . Every good tree bears good fruit, but the bad tree bears bad fruit." He teaches that the deeds, the outcomes in action, are the test of whether a tree is good. Some people reverse the emphasis, putting all their emphasis on the inner being of a person and not on outer action. They say, "Make the inner self good, and good outer actions will follow naturally." There is, of course, some truth to this. But the danger is then splitting the inner self from outer action and focusing only on the inner. Then a person feels righteous because she or he has a good attitude, even though the person's actions do not differ from anyone else's. Jesus does not split inner self from outer action. Jesus emphasizes the actions as the test of the self. The fruits are the indicator of what the roots are like. The whole tree produces the fruits. It is holistic.

To know God as Holy Spirit is to affirm that *the living God moves freely, unfettered by any nation, institution, or ideology*: "As the heavens are higher than the earth, so are my ways higher than your ways and my thoughts than your thoughts" (Isa. 55:8–9). The sovereign God remains the living, dynamic, eternal Judge and Redeemer. No doctrine, no matter how orthodox; no institution, political or ecclesiastical; no human good will, no matter how pure and moral, can claim to possess God's goodness. National Socialism in Germany claimed to represent the nation's social salvation and demanded the allegiance of the populace. Bonhoeffer and Trocmé recognized this as idolatry. If the living God claims our allegiance, then neither national interest nor ideological commitment suffices to guide us into ethical action. Only the ongoing process of repentance can prepare us to discern and respond to the will of God.

It is clear why an ethic that knows God cannot be identified with some racist, nationalistic, ethnic-cleansing, or wealth-acquiring ideology is much more likely to resist the seduction of "every wind and doctrine, people's trickery, and craftiness in deceitful scheming" by which the ideologies seek to manipulate us into supporting their cause instead of the cause of Christ (Eph. 4:14). Many people were seduced into supporting segregationist practices and customs, but Clarence Jordan, Rosa

Parks, Martin Luther King Jr., and Jimmy Carter among others
were clear that those ways of the world were not God's ways.
Many East Germans were seduced into believing the Soviet
Communist system was powerful and unable to be changed, but
it was the followers of Bonhoeffer and Barth, with their incarnational Trinitarian ethic, who led the people in the Revolution
of the Candles that toppled a dictator and the Berlin Wall, bringing about a nonviolent revolution in which not one person died
but something like justice started to emerge.

Exemplary figures such as Bonhoeffer and Trocmé remind
us that God's will can be known and obeyed in a way that produces good fruit in the world. Their words and actions brought
relief to the persecuted, exposed the shame of an unjust regime, and guided future generations of Christian disciples.
Trocmé went on to teach and promote nonviolent social
strategies through his work with the International Fellowship
of Reconciliation. Bonhoeffer, by dying a martyr's death, left a
lasting testimony to God's final victory over an authoritarian
and militaristic regime. They showed the enduring validity of
the way of Jesus amid changing moral systems. By their fruits
we know them.

I have studied many kinds of ethics and observed how they
perform in the laboratory of history. Again and again it seems
clear that those Christians with an incarnational Trinitarian
ethic of the sort I have described here come through. I think
of Clarence Jordan, who wrote a study book on the Sermon on
the Mount and was as clear as can be about following it in
action—devoting his life to overcoming poverty and racism
in South Georgia well before the civil rights movement—and
who certainly did not identify the culture's ways with God's
will. I think of Martin Luther King Jr., whose ethic was Christ-
centered, who saw God as Lord over all of life and not only the
inner life, and who knew very well not to identify the nation's
status quo with God's will. I think of Muriel Lester and
Dorothy Day, and of Karl Barth resisting Hitler, and of many
others.

I am suggesting that even though we do not know all there is to know, and we do not have the certitude of a universal viewpoint, we can see within our own history what kind of ethic comes through, which is truer because of the fruits it bears.

The key here transcends doing these deeds in order to earn us a ticket into the kingdom. The key is to recognize who Jesus is as the one who reveals God's way to us, as the one who shows us that the reign of God is breaking in through him as mustard seeds and pearls of great price in our lives; the key is to give him our commitment to follow him, and give our trust and loyalty to God and not some other power. As participants in the grace that God is bringing in Jesus, we are to do the deeds that Jesus teaches. Our pledge of allegiance to Jesus is, through him, a pledge of allegiance to God whose presence and deliverance he gives to us. This pledge of allegiance is more than merely words, more than affirming doctrines, more than merely studying what Jesus teaches; it is hearing Jesus' words *and doing them*. The theme throughout these sixteen verses from 7:12–27 is *doing*; the word is repeated ten times (though sometimes translated *produce* or *produces,* or *acts*).

To hear these words and do them means to respond to Jesus as the bringer of God's reign by yielding one's life and loyalty in complete surrender to God, and to live Jesus' teachings by focusing on God's presence delivering us and others from our captivity to ways of self-destruction.[2]

Being religious, or saying the right words, or believing the right doctrines, is not the key. Some people whose faith is quite simple and whose doctrinal knowledge might be quite limited nevertheless do the deeds of Jesus in prayer and in relating to others. It is like Matthew 25:31–46, the passage about the judgment between the sheep and the goats. The sheep did not even know that they fed Jesus when he was hungry, welcomed him when he was an outcast, gave him clothes when he had none, or visited him in prison. Jesus said, in effect, when you did it to the least of these, you did it to me.

STANDING ON THE ROCK
OR SINKING IN THE SAND

Everyone then who hears these words of mine and acts on
them will be like a wise man who built his house on rock.
The rain fell, the floods came, and the winds blew and beat
on that house, but it did not fall, because it had been founded
on rock. And everyone who hears these words of mine and
does not act on them will be like a foolish man who built his
house on sand. The rain fell, and the floods came, and the
winds blew and beat against that house, and it fell—and great
was its fall [Matt. 7:24–28].

Jesus' teaching in this passage is so clear that not much needs to
be said. Building a house on rock is not about working hard in
the construction process, or being clever, or knowing when the
flood is coming. It is about building on the rock. Nothing is said
about any other difference in the two houses. The only difference is what they are built on. Jesus does not demand heroic
deeds or supernatural feats, but deeds of love—the kind that he
teaches, like Matthew 25: aiding those who are hungry, are
excluded, are in prison, or need clothing and basic needs. The
rock is just one thing: hearing Jesus' words and doing them.

Jesus says *these* words *of mine.* He means these words in the
Sermon on the Mount, the words that he himself has taught.
This is also what the Great Commission means in Matthew
28:19–20: "Go therefore and *make disciples* of all nations, baptizing them in the name of the Father, the Son, and the Holy
Spirit, and teaching them to obey everything I have commanded you." The command or imperative in the sentence is to
"make disciples." The climax of the sentence is "teaching them
to obey everything I have commanded you." Making disciples
requires teaching that we do what Jesus teaches. This is the rock.

Once again, we encounter the sand. In Matthew 5:13, salt
that has lost its saltiness (that is, its difference from the world)

and no longer lets its deeds shine in the light so that people give glory to God is good for nothing but to be thrown out and trampled under foot, like sand. In Matthew 7:6, those who put their trust in the world's powers and authorities will be trampled under foot, like the sand. Here, the house that is built on the sand of evasion of the Way of Jesus will sink. The coming of the rains and the floods, and the sinking in the sand, refer to the final judgment.

Those who build their houses on sand are the same as those who take the wide way in the first teaching, not doing the deeds that Jesus teaches. Jesus clearly puts before us two ways. One way leads to life and security, standing on the rock. The other way leads to death and destruction. He is asking each of us to choose. Which way will it be?

CHAPTER ONE: SEEKING GOD'S HOLY PRESENCE ON THE MOUNTAIN

1. Compare Exodus 1:1–3:15 with Matthew 1:18–4:2.
2. Dale C. Allison Jr., *The New Moses: A Matthean Typology.* Minneapolis: Fortress, 1993, pp. 172ff. Allison demonstrates the connection between Matthew 5:1–2 and Moses ascending Sinai in Exodus 19 and 20, in God's presence. For insightful discussion, see also W. D. Davies, *The Setting of the Sermon on the Mount.* Cambridge, England: Cambridge University Press, 1976, pp. 85, 93, 99, 116ff.
3. Ulrich Luz, *Matthew 1–7: A Continental Commentary.* Minneapolis: Augsburg Fortress, 1992, pp. 215, 224.
4. Arland Hultgren, *The Parables of Jesus.* Grand Rapids, Mich.: Eerdmans, 2000, p. 222.
5. Gerhard Lohfink, *Wem Gilt die Bergpredigt? Beitrage zu einer christlichen Ethik.* Freiburg, Ger.: Herder, 1988, p. 25. I follow Lohfink in the next paragraphs.
6. Lohfink (1988), pp. 28–29.
7. Shaynah Neshama, *We Testify.* Longwood, Fla.: Xulon Press: 2005, pp. 65–72.

CHAPTER TWO: PARTICIPATING
WITH JOY IN THE REIGN OF GOD

1. Gordon Fee, "Kingdom of God." In Murray Dempster (ed.), *Called and Empowered: Pentecostal Perspectives on Global Mission.* Peabody, Mass.: Hendrickson, 1992, p. 8.

2. N. T. Wright, *Jesus and the Victory of God.* Minneapolis: Fortress, 1996, p. 221.

3. Luz (1992), p. 157.

4. Mark 9:1; Matt. 4:12–17, 8:11–12, 11:12ff, 16:28; Luke 4:16–21, 9:27, 12:32, 13:28–29, 16:16.

5. Bruce Chilton, *God in Strength: Jesus' Announcement of the Kingdom.* Freistadt, Austria: Plöchl, 1979, p. 277. See also Chilton, *A Galilean Rabbi and His Bible: Jesus' Use of the Interpreted Scripture of His Time.* Wilmington, Del.: Glazier, 1984, pp. 129ff.

6. Isaiah 24:23, 31:14, 40:9, 52:7, 53:10.

7. Bruce Chilton, *Pure Kingdom: Jesus' Vision of God.* Grand Rapids, Mich.: Eerdmans, 1996, pp. 11ff; Chilton and Craig Evans, *Studying the Historical Jesus: Evaluations of the State of Current Research.* Leiden, Neth.: E. J. Grill, 1994, p. 268.

8. For example, Isaiah 13:18; 14:1; 27:11; 30:18; 49:10, 13, 15; 54:7, 8, 10; 55:7; 60:10; 63:7, 15.

9. Glen Stassen and David Gushee, *Kingdom Ethics: Following Jesus in Contemporary Context.* Downers Grove, Ill.: InterVarsity, 2003, pp. 41–43.

10. What follows in text is adapted from meditations I wrote for *Hunger for the Word: Lectionary Reflections on Food and Justice: Year B,* Larry Hollar (ed.). Collegeville, Minn.: Liturgical Press, 2005.

CHAPTER THREE: THE BEATITUDES

1. The comparison is adapted from W. D. Davies and Dale C. Allison Jr., *Critical and Exegetical Commentary on the Gospel According to St. Matthew.* Edinburgh: T. & T. Clark, 1988, pp. 436–440. Robert Guelich developed this insight in

articles he published, and then in his book *The Sermon on the Mount* (Dallas: Word, 1982).

2. Pinchas Lapide, *The Sermon on the Mount: Utopia or Program for Action?* Maryknoll, N.Y.: Orbis, 1986, p. 27.

3. F. Brown, S. R. Driver, and C. A. Briggs, *The New Brown, Driver, and Briggs Hebrew and English Lexicon of the Old Testament.* Lafayette, Calif.: Associated Publishers, 1981, p. 776.

4. Guelich (1982), pp. 69, 75.

5. Guelich (1982), pp. 68–69.

6. Hagner, D., *Matthew 1–13.* Dallas: Word, 1993, p. 92.

7. Clarence Jordan, *The Sermon on the Mount* (rev. ed.). Valley Forge, Pa.: Judson, 1974, p. 22.

8. Jordan (1974), p. 23.

9. Jordan (1974), pp. 24–25.

10. Martin Luther King Jr., *Strength to Love.* Cleveland: Collins-World, 1977, p. 48.

11. Hultgren (2000), p. 122.

12. The italics are in Jordan's original (1974), p. 31.

13. Hultgren (2000), pp. 323–324.

14. Bill McKibben, "The Christian Paradox: How a Faithful Nation Gets Jesus Wrong." *Harper's,* Aug. 2005, p. 36. Just so the example does not lead to disempowering cynicism, I point out that some good folks in Kentucky did successfully take action to accomplish the kind of overdue reform that Governor Riley was trying to achieve in Alabama, and it did fund the Kentucky schools more equitably.

15. Davies and Allison (1988), p. 456.

16. Jordan (1974), p. 33.

17. Hagner (1993), p. 94.

18. Glen Stassen, "The Christian Origin of Human Rights." In Stassen, *Just Peacemaking: Transforming Initiatives for Justice and Peace.* Louisville, Ky.: Westminster John Knox Press, 1992.

19. Glen Stassen, "Healing the Rift Between the Sermon on the Mount and Christian Ethics." *Studies in Christian Ethics.* Dec. 2005, pp. 267–308.

20. David Gushee, *Righteous Gentiles of the Holocaust.* St. Paul: Paragon, 2003.
21. Jordan (1974), p. 37.

CHAPTER FOUR: PRACTICING RECONCILIATION AND KEEPING OUR COVENANTS

1. Andrew Lester, *The Angry Christian: A Theology for Care and Counseling.* Louisville, Ky.: Westminster John Knox Press, 2003.
2. Lester (2003), pp. 163–164.
3. Lester (2003), p. 160.
4. Lester (2003), p. 244.
5. Quoted by Allison (1993), p. 74.
6. Luz (1992), p. 296.
7. Guelich (1982), p. 242, and Amy-Jill Levine in Newsom and Ringe, *Women's Bible Commentary.* Louisville, Ky.: Westminster John Knox, 1992, p. 225, quoted in Allison (1993), p. 72.
8. David Gushee, *Getting Marriage Right: Realistic Counsel for Saving and Strengthening Relationships.* Grand Rapids, Mich.: Baker Books, 2004.
9. Gushee (2004), pp. 165–167.

CHAPTER FIVE: TELLING THE TRUTH, MAKING PEACE, LOVING OUR ENEMIES

1. Dietrich Bonhoeffer, *Ethics.* New York: Touchstone, [1955] 1995, pp. 110–116. See also Bonhoeffer's essay "What Is Meant by 'Telling the Truth'?" in *Ethics,* pp. 358–367.
2. Clarence Jordan, *The Substance of Faith and Other Cotton Patch Sermons* (Dallas Lee, ed.). New York: Association Press, 1972, p. 69. Other New Testament scholars increasingly affirm similar translations.
3. John Howard Yoder, *The Politics of Jesus.* Grand Rapids, Mich.: Eerdmans, 1994, pp. 89–92.

4. Glen Stassen (ed.). *Just Peacemaking: Ten Practices for Abolishing War.* Cleveland: Pilgrim Press, 2004.
5. Glen Stassen, *Just Peacemaking: Transforming Initiatives for Justice and Peace.* Louisville, Ky.: Westminster John Knox, 1992, chapter 5.
6. Stassen (2004), chapters 7 and 8.

CHAPTER SIX: THE PRAYER OF JESUS

1. James Mulholland, *Praying Like Jesus.* San Francisco: HarperSanFrancisco: 2001, chapters 10 and 14.
2. Mulholland (2001), p. 29.
3. Helmut Thielicke, *Our Heavenly Father: Sermons on the Lord's Prayer.* New York: HarperCollins, 1960, pp. 55–66.
4. I recommend the eloquent book *An Ethic for Enemies: Forgiveness in Politics* by Donald Shriver (New York: Oxford University Press, 1995).
5. Most translations say "rescue us from the evil one." But in all the rest of his clear teachings, Jesus never says "the evil one." In Judaism this is never the term used for Satan (see Luz, 1992, p. 385). All my life I have heard my church recite this prayer as "deliver us from evil," so that is how I translate it. There are also good reasons for supporting "rescue us from the evil one." You may choose either way.

CHAPTER SEVEN: INVESTING IN GOD'S REIGN AND RESTORATIVE JUSTICE

1. The Bread for the World Website is www.bread.org. It is an outstanding Christian organization, with specific programs for organizing and worshiping in churches; it has won many victories for the world's hungry in Congress and in White House policy.
2. Guelich (1982), pp. 327–328.
3. Guelich (1982), p. 332.
4. Ronald Sider, *Rich Christians in an Age of Hunger.* Dallas: Word Press, 1997; Sider, *Just Generosity: A New Vision for Overcoming Poverty in America.* Grand Rapids, Mich.: Baker Books, 1999.

5. Sider (1999), pp. 186–187.
6. Ron Sider and Heidi Rolland Unruh, *Churches That Make a Difference*. Grand Rapids, Mich.: Baker Books, 2002.
7. Larry Rasmussen, *Earth Community Earth Ethics*. Maryknoll, N.Y.: Orbis, 1996.
8. Frederick L. Gwynn and Joseph L. Blotner, *Faulkner in the University*. Charlottesville: University of Virginia Press, 1959, pp. 245–246.
9. Rasmussen (1996), p. 59.

CHAPTER EIGHT: FORGOING JUDGMENT FOR FORGIVENESS

1. David Garland, *Reading Matthew*. New York: Crossroad, 1993, pp. 85–86.
2. Dale Allison, *The Sermon on the Mount*. New York: Crossroad, 1999, p. 153; John Stott, *The Message of the Sermon on the Mount*. Downers Grove, Ill.: InterVarsity, 1978, p. 178.
3. Stassen (2004), chapter 4.
4. Bonhoeffer's confession can be read in his *Ethics* ([1955] 1995), pp. 110–119, or in the newer and more accurate translation from Fortress Press, 2005, pp. 134–145.
5. Bonhoeffer ([1955] 1995).
6. Guelich (1982), pp. 352–353.
7. NRSV translates "your brother" as "your neighbor" to avoid gendered language.
8. James E. Dittes, *Bias and the Pious*. Minneapolis: Augsburg, 1973, p. 79. Many sociological studies show this distinction, and Dittes summarizes some of the studies in a highly readable way. See also the sociological study combined with church history of Mennonites in Leo Driedger and Donald Kraybill, *Mennonite Peacemaking*. Scottdale, Pa.: Herald, 1994, pp. 175ff. See also writings of church historian Donald Dayton; and Robert L. Young, "Religious Orientation, Race, and Support for the Death Penalty." In Glen Stassen (ed.), *Capital Punishment*. Cleveland: Pilgrim, 1998, pp. 205–215.

9. Lewis B. Smedes, *Forgive and Forget: Healing the Hurts We Don't Deserve.* San Francisco: HarperSanFrancisco, 1996, p. xv.
10. Smedes (1996), p. 79.
11. Smedes (1996), p. 79.
12. Smedes (1996), p. 108.
13. Smedes (1996), pp. 106–107.
14. Smedes (1996), pp. xiii, 71, 94, 102, 143.
15. Smedes (1996), p. 147.

CHAPTER NINE: PRACTICING LOYALTY TO GOD, NOT TO WORLDLY POWERS

1. I want to thank Ched Myers, author of *Binding the Strong Man* (Maryknoll, N.Y.: Orbis, 1988, pp. 190–191), for his insights about the herd of pigs rushing into the sea.
2. Jim Wallis, *The Call to Conversion* (rev. and updated). San Francisco: HarperSanFrancisco, 2005a.
3. Wallis (2005a), pp. 3–4.
4. Wallis (2005a), pp. 5–6.
5. Wallis (2005a), pp. 13, 17–18.
6. Jim Wallis, *God's Politics: Why the Right Gets It Wrong and the Left Doesn't Get It.* San Francisco: HarperSanFrancisco, 2005b, p. xiv.
7. Wallis (2005b), p. 4.

CHAPTER TEN: HOW TO TELL A TRUE ETHIC FROM A FALSE ONE

1. I want to thank G. Scott Becker for his contribution to the paragraphs in this section. This is a modified form of an article we wrote together about Dietrich Bonhoeffer for the one-hundredth anniversary of Bonhoeffer's birth.
2. Guelich (1982), p. 413.

FOR FURTHER READING

ABOUT THE GOSPEL OF MATTHEW AND THE SERMON ON THE MOUNT

Allison Jr., Dale. *The Sermon on the Mount.* New York: Crossroad, 1999.

Davies, W. D., and D. C. Allison Jr. *Critical and Exegetical Commentary on the Gospel According to St. Matthew.* Edinburgh: T. & T. Clark, 1988, pp. 436–440.

Garland, David. *Reading Matthew.* New York: Crossroad, 1993, pp. 85–86.

Guelich, Robert. *The Sermon on the Mount.* Dallas: Word, 1982.

Hagner, Donald. *Matthew 1–13.* Dallas: Word, 1993.

Jordan, Clarence. *The Sermon on the Mount* (rev. ed.). Valley Forge, Pa.: Judson, 1974.

Lapide, Pinchas. *The Sermon on the Mount: Utopia or Program for Action?* Maryknoll, N.Y.: Orbis, 1986.

Luz, Ulrich. *Matthew 1–7: A Continental Commentary.* Minneapolis: Augsburg Fortress, 1992.

Mulholland, James. *Praying Like Jesus.* San Francisco: HarperSanFrancisco, 2001.

Stott, John. *The Message of the Sermon on the Mount.* Downers Grove, Ill.: InterVarsity, 1978.

ABOUT JESUS' PARABLES

Hultgren, Arland. *The Parables of Jesus.* Grand Rapids, Mich.:
Eerdmans, 2000.

TESTIMONIES OF GOD'S PRESENT ACTION

Dempster, Murray (ed.). *Called and Empowered: Pentecostal
Perspectives on Global Mission.* Peabody, Mass.: Hendrickson,
1992.

Hollar, Larry (ed.). *Hunger for the Word: Lectionary Reflections on
Food and Justice: Year B.* Collegeville, Minn.: Liturgical Press,
2005.

Neshama, Shaynah. *We Testify.* Longwood, Fla.: Xulon Press, 2005.

THE LIFE AND TEACHINGS
OF THE HISTORICAL JESUS

Bockmuehl, Marcus. *This Jesus: Martyr, Lord, Messiah.* Downers
Grove, Ill.: InterVarsity Press, 1994.

Borg, Marcus. *Conflict, Holiness and Politics in the Teachings of Jesus.*
Harrisburg, Penn.: Trinity Press International, 1998.

Borg, Marcus, and N. T. Wright. *The Meaning of Jesus: Two Visions.*
San Francisco: HarperSanFrancisco, 2000.

Chilton, Bruce. *God in Strength: Jesus' Announcement of the Kingdom.*
Freistadt, Austria: Plöchl, 1979.

Chilton, Bruce. *A Galilean Rabbi and His Bible: Jesus' Use of the
Interpreted Scripture of His Time.* Wilmington, Del.: Glazier,
1984.

Herzog, William. *Jesus, Justice, and the Reign of God.* Louisville, Ky.:
Westminster John Knox, 2000.

Marshall, Chris. *The Little Book of Biblical Justice.* Intercourse, Pa.:
Good Books, 2005.

Wright, N. T. *Jesus and the Victory of God.* Minneapolis: Fortress,
1996.

Wright, N. T. *The Challenge of Jesus: Rediscovering Who Jesus Was and Is.* Downers Grove, Ill.: InterVarsity Press, 1999.

Yoder, John Howard. *The Politics of Jesus.* Grand Rapids, Mich.: Eerdmans, 1994.

CHRISTIAN ETHICS AS FOLLOWING JESUS

Dittes, James E. *Bias and the Pious.* Minneapolis: Augsburg, 1973.

Fillingim, David. *Extreme Virtues: Living on the Prophetic Edge.* Scottdale, Pa., and Waterloo, Ont.: Herald Press, 2003.

Gushee, David. *Righteous Gentiles of the Holocaust.* St. Paul: Paragon, 2003.

Gushee, David. *Getting Marriage Right: Realistic Counsel for Saving and Strengthening Relationships.* Grand Rapids, Mich.: Baker Books, 2004.

King Jr., Martin Luther. *Strength to Love.* Minneapolis: Fortress Press, 1981.

Lester, Andrew. *The Angry Christian: A Theology for Care and Counseling.* Louisville, Ky.: Westminster John Knox Press, 2003.

Marshall, Christopher. *Beyond Retribution: A New Testament Vision for Justice, Crime, and Punishment.* Grand Rapids, Mich.: Eerdmans, 2001.

Marshall, Christopher. *Crowned with Glory and Honor: Human Rights in the Biblical Tradition.* Telford, Pa.: Pandora Press, 2001.

Rasmussen, Larry. *Earth Community Earth Ethics.* Maryknoll, N.Y.: Orbis, 1996.

Shriver, Donald. *An Ethic for Enemies: Forgiveness in Politics.* Oxford: Oxford University Press, 1995.

Shriver, Donald. *Honest Patriots: Loving a Country Enough to Remember Its Misdeeds.* Oxford: Oxford University Press, 2005.

Sider, Ronald. *Rich Christians in an Age of Hunger.* Dallas: Word Press, 1997.

Sider, Ronald. *Just Generosity: A New Vision for Overcoming Poverty in America.* Grand Rapids, Mich.: Baker Books, 1999.

Sider, Ronald, and Heidi Rolland Unruh. *Churches That Make a Difference.* Grand Rapids, Mich.: Baker Books, 2002.

Smedes, Lewis B. *Forgive and Forget: Healing the Hurts We Don't Deserve.* San Francisco: HarperSanFrancisco, 1996.

Stassen, Glen (ed.). *Just Peacemaking: Transforming Initiatives for Justice and Peace.* Louisville, Ky.: Westminster John Knox Press, 1992.

Stassen, Glen (ed.). *Just Peacemaking: Ten Practices for Abolishing War.* Cleveland: Pilgrim Press, 2004.

Thurman, Howard. *Jesus and the Disinherited.* Richmond, Ind.: Friends United Press, 1981.

Wallis, Jim. *The Call to Conversion* (revised and updated). San Francisco: HarperSanFrancisco, 2005.

Wallis, Jim. *God's Politics: Why the Right Gets It Wrong and the Left Doesn't Get It.* San Francisco: HarperSanFrancisco, 2005.

Glen H. Stassen is Lewis B. Smedes Professor of Christian Ethics at Fuller Theological Seminary in Pasadena, California. He has written several books in Christian ethics, including *Just Peacemaking*, and (with David P. Gushee) he won *Christianity Today's* award for the best book of the year in theology or ethics for *Kingdom Ethics: Following Jesus in Contemporary Context*. He invites you to peruse more about his interests and other stuff at www.fuller.edu/sot/faculty/stassen.

INDEX

Greed: traditional teaching against, 126

Guelich, R., 43–44, 75, 153

Gushee, D., 78–80

H

Habitat for Humanity, 46

Hagner, D., 57

Healing: of blindness, 149; as a characteristic of the Reign of God, 25, 30–32; as a sign of God's presence, 11–15

Hitler, A., 59–60, 152, 193–194, 198

Honecker, E., 96

Hultgren, A., 51

Human Immunodeficiency Virus (HIV): prevention of, 131

I

Idealism: and interpretations of Jesus' teachings, 15–16, 40–43, 56–57, 63, 65, 97, 186–188

Incarnational ethics, 195–198

Inter-faith dialogue, 182–183

International Baptist Theological Seminary, 7

International Fellowship of Reconciliation, 198

Isaiah: on delivering justice, 127, 130; on the Fatherhood of God, 112–113; on misplaced loyalties, 177; prophecies of fulfilled in Jesus, 8–11, 15, 44; references to in the Beatitudes, 41–44, 48, 52, 54, 57; the Reign of God in, 21–36, 109

J

Jesus Prayer. *See* Prayer of Jesus

John the Baptist: arrest of, 22; message of, 5–6, 10, 19

Jordan, C., 45–49, 54, 57, 62, 89, 197–198

Joy: as a characteristic of the Reign of God, 20, 25, 30–32, 35–37; descriptions of in Beatitudes, 38–45, 48, 51, 54, 56–59

Jubilee: descriptions of in the Beatitudes, 41–43, 54–55

Jubilee 2000, 54–55

Judging: and self-justification, 148–151, 155–156; traditional teaching against, 146–148

Just peacemaking: practices of, 95–98, 102–104. *See also* Peacemaking

Justice: as a characteristic of the Reign of God, 25, 29–30, 32–37, 50, 61; as deliverance or restoration, 9–11, 32–37, 51–55, 58–59, 125–143; as fairness, 32–37; for the poor, 125–135, 170, 179–181; as retribution, 35

K

Kern Road Mennonite Church, South Bend, Indiana, 180

Khan, A. G., 96

King, M. L., Jr., 50–51, 92, 96–97, 175–176, 181, 197–198

Kingdom of God. *See* Reign of God

Koinonia Farm, 45–46

L

Laplace, P. S. de, 6–7

Le Chambon, France: rescue of Jews in, 194–195

Lester, A., 68–69

Lester, M., 196

Levine, A., 75

familiarity of, 106; and the
Fatherhood of God, 110–113;
and forgiveness, 121–122, 146–
148, 155; and the name of God,
113–116; as organizing center of
the Sermon on the Mount, 109–
111; and the Reign of God, 19,
116–119; and temptation, 122–
124, 172; and the will of God,
119–120
Prodigal Son: parable of, 58, 147, 169

Q
Qumran, 60

R
Racial Segregation, 45–47, 197–198.
See also Civil Rights Movement
Rasmussen, L., 137, 142
Reconciliation: between spouses,
76–80; as a transforming initia-
tive, 64, 67–70
Rees, H., 148
Reign of God: characteristics of,
8–11, 21, 17–37, 50, 116–119,
177, 191, 193. *See also* Beatitudes,
Deliverance, God, Healing, Joy,
Justice, Peace, Prayer of Jesus,
Return from exile
Repentance: collective, 151–153; as
a community practice, 154; and
the Reign of God, 29, 47, 117,
119, 151, 177; as a shift in loyalty,
176–181. *See also* Conversion
Restorative Justice. *See* Justice
Retaliation: law of, 89–90
Return from exile: as a characteristic
of the Reign of God, 25–28,
30–32

Revenge: and forgiveness, 160–163;
as vicious cycle, 89–91
Righteousness. *See* Justice
Riley, B., 55

S
Sabbath, observance of, 4
Save the Children, 94
Salvation. *See* Deliverance
Self-justification, 148–151
Sider, R., 133–135
Smedes, L., 158–164
Solidarity Movement: in Poland, 96
Stassen, D., 15, 30–31, 122–123
Stott, J., 149

T
Temptation: deliverance from, 122–
124; of Jesus, 10–11; sexual, 71–
75
Ten Commandments, 2–4, 64, 71,
83, 114–115, 119
Terrorism: and love for enemies, 102
Theilicke, H., 118–119
Theis, R., 195
Transforming initiatives: of covenant
keeping, 76–81; of giving trust
and loyalty to God, 168, 170–
172; of investing in justice,
128–129, 132–135; of love for
neighbor and enemy, 99, 101–
104; of nonviolent surprise,
90–98; of reconciliation, 64,
67–70, 76–80; of repentance and
mutual correction, 145, 151–154;
of responsibility and respect,
72, 74–75; of secret acts of righteousness, 107–109; of truth-
telling, 84, 86–88